The Inside St

27/6

FOURTEEN MAY DAYS

The Inside Story of the Loyalist Strike of 1974

Don Anderson

GILL & MACMILLAN

Published in Ireland by
Gill & Macmillan Ltd
Goldenbridge
Dublin 8
with associated companies throughout the world
© Don Anderson 1994
0 7171 2177 1
Print origination by Seton Music Graphics Ltd,
Bantry, Co. Cork
Printed by ColourBooks Ltd, Dublin

A catalogue record is available for this book from the British Library.

1   3   5   4   2

All photographs in this book are
reproduced by kind permission of
the *Belfast Telegraph*.

To Rosey, Kiera and Arran

CONTENTS

Foreword by Martin Dillon   ix

Preface   xi

List of Abbreviations   xiii

Chapter One   1

Chapter Two   12

Chapter Three   18

Chapter Four   33

Chapter Five   40

Chapter Six   51

Chapter Seven   62

Chapter Eight   68

Chapter Nine   87

Chapter Ten   97

Chapter Eleven   107

Chapter Twelve   116

Chapter Thirteen   124

Chapter Fourteen   134

Conclusion   146

Appendix A: *The Sunningdale Agreement*   158

Appendix B: *Members of the Northern Ireland Assembly*   165

Appendix C: *Sample of Minutes of the UWC Co-ordinating Committee*   169

Index   172

FOREWORD

The modern rebellion of 1974 is one of the most significant—
and intriguing—events of the last 25 years of conflict. Many
writers have either failed to detect the significance of those
fourteen days, or have dealt with them in a cursory fashion. It
was an episode of complex political, social and military events,
which have not been unravelled until the arrival of this book.

The rebellion, by a large section of the loyalist and Unionist
community, is a landmark in the history of the period. Its rele-
vance to present-day events cannot be dismissed, and must be
one of the factors which will be central to any analysis of the
political way forward. British government will ignore it at their
peril.

Don Anderson provides us, writers and historians alike, with
penetrating insights into the personalities of the period, and the
intricacy of the political machinations which led to the collapse
of the most far-reaching political process since the setting up of
the Northern Ireland state. He brings to this account the inves-
tigative skills of an accomplished journalist and the lively writing
style of the novelist. He presents us with a contemporaneous
account which, by its very nature, is closer to reality than any
previous portrayal of those events.

This is a book which both historians and students of modern
history will find invaluable when they come to write about the
period. It is an exciting window into the past which illuminates
both the strains and stresses within Unionism, and the vulner-
ability of the constitutional link. It presents the risks facing any
British government seeking to initiate a settlement which con-
fronts the basic instincts and aspirations of a large section of the
Protestant community. At a time when the Dublin and London
governments are searching for a political framework, and some
are advocating a return to the power-sharing experiment with
an Irish dimension, there is no better manuscript than this one

to make us aware of the inherent risks in the volatile politics of Northern Ireland.

After reading this book, some of us may be forced to conclude that the rebellion, known as the Workers' Council Strike, was one of the major factors in conditioning the politics of the last 20 years. It made clear to Harold Wilson and successive British prime ministers that Unionists held more than just a political veto on any future settlement.

MARTIN DILLON

PREFACE

A FIRST WORD

I have called this book an anecdotal history because it does not pretend to be anything as grand as an academic study, a thesis or a monograph. It is a simple account of an extraordinary fortnight in May 1974, a fortnight which set the political agenda on the subject of Northern Ireland for Northern Ireland itself, for the United Kingdom and for the Republic of Ireland.

History is a succession of landmark events, each modifying what has passed before. Ireland is still bound by the effects of the Battle of the Boyne in 1690, modified by Catholic emancipation, land wars and the famine. Modified by Home Rule Bills, by the 1916 Easter Rising, the foundation of the Irish Free State, partition of the island. By the Unionist government in Stormont, by Ireland's 1937 constitution, by the Civil Rights Movement, by the onslaught of the Provisional IRA and by an Ulster Protestant backlash: that fortnight in May 1974.

The book is based on a document I wrote immediately after the Ulster Workers' Council strike. Listed alphabetically, the principal sources were the following people, all of whom I had known through my job as a television and radio reporter: Glen Barr, UWC strike leader; Roy Bradford, Executive Minister; George Chambers, general manager, Northern Ireland Milk Marketing Board; Austin Currie, Executive Minister; Paddy Devlin, Executive Minister; Brian Faulkner, Executive Chief Minister; Gerry Fitt, Deputy Chief Minister; Brian Garrett, Northern Ireland Labour Party; John Hume, Executive Minister; Alison Lennox, Belfast oil refinery manager; Harry Murray, chairman of the Ulster Workers' Council; Oliver Napier, Executive Minister; Bob Pagels, Ulster Workers' Council; Hugo Patterson, Northern Ireland Electricity spokesman; Sandy Scott, Chief Shop Steward at the Harland and Wolff shipyard; Jim Smith, technical director, Northern Ireland Electricity Service; Andy Tyrie, leader of the Ulster Defence Association.

My story makes no pretence at being comprehensive, or the truth and nothing but the truth in approved courtroom manner. Suspect any historian, anecdotal or otherwise, who proclaims such. However, the manuscript retains the flavours of the time and only in the concluding chapter have I allowed myself the distortion of hindsight, which contains the flavours of nearly twenty years on. Everything in this book is fact or at least fiction believed in good faith to be fact. Since we are destined to learn from neither, it scarcely matters which is which.

Read history for entertainment.

I received many kindnesses in the preparation of this book, not least encouragement from a large number of friends. In particular I am very grateful for hard work by lawyer Brian Garrett and journalist Rupert Millar. Any shortcomings in the manuscript are not to be laid at their doors, but at my own.

DON ANDERSON
Spring 1994

LIST OF ABBREVIATIONS

AEU	Amalgamated Engineering Union
BBC	British Broadcasting Corporation
CSE	Certificate of Secondary Education
DOW	Down Orange Welfare
DUP	Democratic Unionist Party
GOC	General Officer Commanding (British Army)
IRA	Irish Republican Army (usually refers to Provisional IRA)
LAW	Loyalist Association of Workers
MP	Member of Parliament
NIES	Northern Ireland Electricity Service
NILP	Northern Ireland Labour Party
OIEC	Oil Industry Emergency Committee
OV	Orange Volunteers
RAF	Royal Air Force
RTE	Radio Telefís Éireann
SDLP	Social Democratic and Labour Party
TUC	Trades Union Congress
UDA	Ulster Defence Association
USC	Ulster Service Corps
USCA	Ulster Special Constabulary Association
UUUC	United Ulster Unionist Council
UVF	Ulster Volunteer Force
UVSC	Ulster Volunteer Service Corps
UWC	Ulster Workers' Council

ONE

It was just after six o'clock in the evening of Tuesday 14 May 1974. A series of events had just taken place inside the impressive Stormont Parliament building on the outskirts of Belfast. As so often happens, the full significance of what was unfolding was largely lost on participants and witnesses.

From that time, on that date and at that place a countdown lasting fourteen days began at the end of which a helpless British government had capitulated to the Protestants of Northern Ireland, or in the words of an extremely angry Prime Minister at the time, to 'people who spend their lives sponging on Westminster and British democracy and who systematically assault democratic methods'.

This is the story of the last days of the most ambitious political experiment ever attempted in troubled Northern Ireland: a coalition of Protestants and Catholics, of partitionist and anti-partitionist politicians in a government at Stormont in Belfast.

If the story had unfolded in the pages of an intricate political thriller, the author would have been accused of stretching credulity too far. Events began with a mere handful of men riddled with doubts and uncertainties but who triggered one of the most extraordinary, most effective—and shortest—rebellions in British history. The Ulster Workers' Council (UWC) strike, as it came to be known, brought an intricate modern economy and way of life to a screeching halt, reducing government to impotence in the space of a few days. This is something the Provisional IRA has never come near to achieving in over twenty years of terror, assassination and guerrilla warfare.

One of those UWC organisers was a shortish middle-aged Belfast shipyard worker, Harry Murray. At six o'clock on 14 May, inside that Stormont building and at the conclusion of a particular debate in the Northern Ireland Assembly, Harry Murray announced to a clutch of journalists that a general strike was to begin the following day.

The journalists reported his statement but without conviction. Few gave credence to the Ulster Workers' Council in whose name the strike had been called. Many observers openly doubted its existence. Murray himself had hardly been convincing the previous day on local television when he talked of 'between fifty and eighty thousand workers' as the membership. Proper organisations know their membership within more precise limits.

Harry Murray was a moral and religious man with whom half truths, even in a just cause, sat uneasily. Murray knew the truth about the UWC. He knew that its 21-member executive committee, drawn in theory from all six counties of the province, existed only on paper and had never met.

As a mass movement, the UWC did not exist.

Murray was relying on the efforts of a very small number of fellow organisers in key industries, relying on the hopes of a spontaneous surge of support from the body of Protestant workers, and—though he hardly dared admit the fact even to himself—upon the actions of Protestant paramilitary organisations.

That May evening the politicians streamed past Murray towards the car parks at Stormont with no sense of foreboding. They largely ignored Murray. Indeed most would not have recognised him.

Yet in a few days they came to know Murray's face very well as he and his committee usurped huge areas of control from government. Reporters came from other continents to record and publish his words. The Prime Minister of the United Kingdom himself would make a ministerial broadcast to the nation in furious and bitter reaction to Murray and his associates.

Murray and his colleagues were to end up winning the day, causing the collapse of a major plank of British policy in Ireland.

But that day in Stormont Murray was a nobody. He followed the politicians out of the gates of Stormont and went home to his wife. He told her simply, 'It's on.'

But it was not 'on'. The strike call went largely unheeded the following day, and to understand why requires an understanding of how badly the Protestants had used the strike weapon up to that date. Just over a year prior to this, in February 1973, the Protestants had attempted another general strike. They knew that in theory a strike by every Protestant in a province that was sixty-five per cent Protestant should have massive impact. But the 1973 strike had descended into an embarrassing and violent shambles.

Small wonder Murray said a special prayer that May night.

By the beginning of summer 1974 few Protestants retained much faith in political strikes. The February 1973 strike was a debacle, causing so much senseless violence that it hardly seemed credible that anyone would consider the tactic again. The 1973 strike goes a long way towards explaining why scant attention was paid to Murray's announcement, and why Murray and others alongside him privately nursed doubts.

On Wednesday 7 February 1973 the United Loyalist Council led by William Craig had called a one-day general strike. In a 24-hour period, five people were shot dead and seven wounded by gunfire. One of those killed was a fireman tackling a fire in Sandy Row itself, the very heart of Protestant Belfast. The police said at the time that the unfortunate fireman had been shot deliberately to prevent the fire being put out.

This particular killing more than others had horrified the ordinary Protestant upon whose support the strike organisers were depending, but the other chaos and disorder further undermined the strikers. There were eight explosions and thirty-five malicious fires, many the results of attacks on Catholic property, including churches.

Violence of this nature and scale made nonsense of claims by loyalist politicians, including William Craig himself, that the essential ingredient of 'Protestant gut reaction' was not sectarian.

February 1973 also provoked exchanges of gunfire, not just between Protestant and Catholic parts of Belfast, but more significantly between Protestant gunmen and British troops. It was hard at that time to reconcile the term 'loyalist' with a loyalty that involved Protestant guns being turned upon the forces of the crown.

Harold Wilson, leader of the Labour opposition at Westminster (who would be Prime Minister during the 1974 strike) commented bitterly that the time had come to end the widespread use of the word 'loyalist' as normally applied in Ulster. He was supporting the then Conservative Secretary of State for Northern Ireland, William Whitelaw. Whitelaw declared that the responsibility for the violence rested squarely on the loyalists.

It was a most uncomfortable position for many Protestants, whose basic political philosophy was the maintenance of the union with Great Britain. Such unmerciful bipartisan condemnation from London was normally reserved for the Provisional and Official IRA.

The outrage of the 1973 strike was the degree of intimidation suffered by many Protestants at the hands of other Protestants to prevent them travelling to work or to chase them from work.

In short this strike had set Protestant upon Protestant, had besmirched the name of the Ulster Protestant inside and outside the province and had drawn attention once again to an aspect of loyalism that bore frightening similarities to the IRA and its violence.

The broad aim of the 1973 strike was to re-establish some kind of Protestant or loyalist control over affairs in the province, especially over security policy. That control had been lost in March 1972 when the Westminster government dismissed the Unionist government in Belfast and suspended the Stormont parliament. The Unionists under their leader, Brian Faulkner, had refused to agree to give up law and order powers and Westminster replied by collapsing Unionist rule in the province and establishing direct rule.

The Protestants smarted. The wound of losing their Stormont cut deep.

To the Protestants, whether they termed themselves Unionists or loyalists, direct rule from London was a political blow of major proportions. It led to a great intensification of Unionist distrust of all London politicians. Westminster in their eyes was soft on the IRA, a suspicion which deepened considerably when the Northern Ireland Secretary secretly met IRA leaders in an abortive conclave in London in July 1972.

A range of Protestant feeling from misgiving to open hostility to the national government in London is central to an understanding of why the 1973 strike happened and why, despite its violent failure, another political stoppage was being attempted in May 1974.

After the 1973 strike, events in Northern Ireland had moved comparatively fast. On 20 March 1973 the Westminster government published a White Paper proposing an assembly at Stormont, elected by proportional representation but with internal security remaining firmly in central government control.

But the quarrel over who should control security in the province quickly faded into the background in the face of a radical proposal in the White Paper that Protestants and Catholics, Unionists and anti-Unionists, find enough common ground to unite in a coalition administration at Stormont. Moreover, there should be acknowledgment of both a British and Irish dimension in the government of Northern Ireland.

For many traditional Protestants and Ulster Unionists, there could be no compromise between those who wanted to be British and those who wanted to be Irish. Compromise was viewed in British politics as a respectable political process; in Ireland, in particular among Northern Ireland loyalists, it has connotations of betrayal.

Ranged against the Unionists was the Social Democratic and Labour Party (the SDLP) which represented the majority of Catholics and, crucially, believed that compromise was possible. Under its leader Gerry Fitt, MP for West Belfast, its policy was to work towards the eventual unity of Ireland by consent. It was able therefore to welcome the ideas of partnership government along with some kind of cross-border institution to give substance to the Irish dimension.

The SDLP signalled that if the Unionists would compromise, it would put the achievement of an Irish unitary state on the long finger. The big question was whether the Unionists, or enough of them, could compromise and admit Catholics into office in Stormont government. Clearly there were some Protestants who would do so and they demonstrated the fact by leaving the Unionist Party and joining the cross-bench Alliance Party. The Alliance Party, led by Oliver Napier, drew its support from moderate Protestants and Catholics on a platform of partnership and reconciliation—and compromise.

But other Unionists had also left the monolithic Unionist Party because of their opposition to reforms already wrested from Unionists in the last years of the old Stormont government. Broadly speaking they were against compromise. These splinter Unionists were the Democratic Unionist Party (the DUP) under the Rev. Ian Paisley, and the Vanguard Unionist Progressive Party led by William Craig.

In the rump of the old pan-Unionist party, which between 1921 and 1972 usually held about three-quarters of the seats in the old Stormont parliament, the strains imposed by recent events had become intolerable by 1973.

The party was obviously split by the time of the local council elections in May 1973. Candidates were calling themselves either Unionists or Official Unionists in an election which was a foretaste of what was to happen the following month, when an election was held for a 78-seat assembly under the White Paper proposals.

The Unionist Party fought the assembly election of 28 June in startling disarray. There were unofficial Unionists against the White Paper proposals and others supporting it under the same party label. There were official Unionists similarly divided. Brian Faulkner, leader of the party, was regarded as pro-White Paper even though his manifesto stated, 'Unionists are not prepared to participate in government with those whose primary objective is to break the union with Great Britain'. He was regarded as pro-White Paper because he would never say publicly whether he believed the primary objective of the Catholic and anti-Unionist SDLP was the breaking of the link with Great Britain. Faulkner, a keen horseman, was no less expert at straddling more than one political mount.

It is less confusing therefore to disregard the election labels of the Unionists and express the result on the Protestant side as follows. The pro-Faulkner pro-White Paper Unionists won twenty seats. Anti-White Paper Unionists won twelve seats.

Ian Paisley's Democratic Unionists (against the White Paper) gained eight seats, William Craig's Vanguard Unionists seven seats and other loyalists opposing the White Paper and power sharing, three seats.

On the Protestant side of the house therefore, more seats fell to those opposing the White Paper and power sharing—a important factor. However, the SDLP on the Catholic side had nineteen seats. Together with the Faulkner Unionists they could form a coalition with majority support in the assembly. With the added support of eight Alliance members, such a coalition would have a safe working majority.

The Conservative administration in London therefore presented the prospect of a devolved government once more at Stormont—albeit without security powers—if these parties could agree to coalition.

A coalition agreement was never a foregone conclusion. As the assembly election had demonstrated, a very large section of the Protestant population was frightened by the idea of Catholic ministers. On the Catholic side, the SDLP had withdrawn from the old Stormont parliament, had instituted a rent and rates strike in protest at internment without trial and had refused to take part in the Darlington conference which had laid the groundwork for the White Paper proposals. Even the attitude of the Faulkner Unionists could best be described as ambivalent.

Power sharing might have been yet another stillborn idea but for the patience and skill of the Northern Ireland Secretary, William Whitelaw, who secured agreement eventually in November 1973. The following month, the Sunningdale conference was convened in the Sunningdale Civil Service College in Berkshire. At this conference the Faulkner Unionists, the SDLP and the Alliance parties, together with representatives of the governments in Dublin and London, put together an outline agreement. Ratification by the new Northern Ireland assembly was planned to follow.

In brief outline (full text in appendix A), the agreement safeguarded the position of Northern Ireland as part of the United Kingdom as long as the majority wished; a cross-border Council of Ireland was to be set up with an advisory assembly and with a 14-member council of ministers which could only act by unanimous decision. The agreement provided for later arrangements to make it more difficult for criminals to escape justice in any part of the island by dodging across the border. The United Kingdom promised to end detention without trial as soon as circumstances permitted and further promised to give the new Stormont government increased powers over matters such as policing once the administration was seen to be working coherently.

The fishbone in the gullet for Unionists, even many Faulkner Unionists, was the idea of a Council of Ireland. Through it the claim of the Republic of Ireland to have an interest in the affairs of Northern Ireland was being recognised, not only by the United Kingdom but by the Unionist signatories at Sunningdale. Privately, even though the arrangements for such a Council of Ireland gave the participating Unionist the power of veto, the SDLP were amazed at how much they had achieved. The SDLP would have settled for less.

In cold logic, if ever politics allows it, the Unionists had castrated the envisaged Council of Ireland by the veto provision. But impressions in politics are everything. Many Unionists had only to hear the name of the body to be opposed to it.

On 1 January 1974 the new Northern Ireland Executive was sworn in by a newly appointed Conservative Northern Ireland Secretary, Francis Pym. They were: Chief Executive, Brian Faulkner (Unionist); Deputy Chief Executive, Gerry Fitt (SDLP); Legal Minister and Head of the Office of Law Reform, Oliver Napier, (Alliance); Minister of Information, John Baxter (Unionist): Minister of the Environment, Roy Bradford (Unionist); Minister of Housing, Local Government and Planning, Austin Currie (SDLP); Minister of Health and Social Service, Paddy Devlin (SDLP); Minister of Commerce, John Hume (SDLP); Minister of Finance, Herbert Kirk (Unionist); Minister of Education, Basil McIvor (Unionist); Minister of Agriculture, Leslie Morrell (Unionist).

Four other ministers were part of the administration but not in the Executive itself: Ivan Cooper (SDLP), community relations; Edward McGrady (SDLP), planning and co-ordination; Robert Cooper (Alliance), manpower services; Major Lloyd Hall-Thompson (Unionist), Chief Whip.

As the press cameras whirred and flashed, the new ministers shook hands with each other and smiled confidently. They knew that this new Executive had tensions within it, but given time to gain a common experience in power, given time to show the sullen and angry loyalists that their worst fears were groundless, given time to convince the doubting SDLP voters that their party leaders had not become 'Castle Catholics', given time to gain the confidence of London and Dublin, this bold move might just be represented by historians as the beginning of the end of Ireland's long troubles.

Such hopes were not misplaced optimism. Catholics seemed likely to give the Executive and the Sunningdale arrangements a chance. The loyalist parties—Paisley's Democratic Unionists, Craig's Vanguard Unionists and the anti-Sunningdale Unionists led by Harry West—seemed unable to unite to form the more effective political opposition. They appeared to give substance to the old jest that if you put a dozen Protestant Ulstermen together you would end up with twelve political parties and twelve religions.

But very quickly the anti-Sunningdale faction of the Unionist Party cleared the decks for action. On 4 January, only a few days after the installation of the new power-sharing Executive, a conference of Faulkner's own party members rejected the Sunningdale agreement by 427 votes to 374. Faulkner resigned the leadership of the Unionist Party and Harry West from Fermanagh stepped into his shoes.

If the Unionist Party had been a normal coherent political party, this event in itself should have brought down the Executive. However, the Unionist Party had effectively split during the elections and Faulkner simply continued as Chief Executive with the support of his Faulkner Unionists in the assembly. The West Unionists, or Official Unionists as they could now term themselves, had only twelve assembly members but they controlled the party machine and headquarters.

Nevertheless the fact that the Unionist Party, the party of government for fifty years in Northern Ireland, the party of the Protestant establishment and ascendency, the party still regarded by the majority of Protestants as the respectable and dominant representation of their cause and beliefs—the fact that this party had been abandoned by Faulkner and his faction weakened Faulkner's political base considerably.

Almost immediately Harry West led his Official Unionist Party into coalition with the Democratic and Vanguard Unionists against Sunningdale. This brought into being the United Ulster Unionist Council (UUUC) under the collective leadership of West, Paisley and Craig. The united loyalists were thus prepared on 22 January 1974 for the first meeting at Stormont of the new assembly with Faulkner as the Chief Executive.

Their first action was to rob the occasion of any dignity. When the Speaker of the assembly, Nat Minford, took the chair he found that the front bench to his right was occupied by UUUC members in defiance of an assembly resolution. That bench was reserved for the Executive. The Speaker ordered them to vacate the front bench. Paisley replied by trying to make a point of order, a move the Speaker persistently rejected. Meanwhile the UUUC showed no sign of giving up their occupancy of the front bench. There was general uproar and worse to follow. The Official Report of Debates minutes the beginning of the Executive's parliamentary life as follows:

Mr Speaker: If the Honourable members will not obey my Ruling then I must ask them to withdraw immediately from the Chamber for the remainder of this day's sitting.

Rev. Dr Paisley: You have forty armoured cars of the British Army to help you.

Mr Speaker: The Sergeant-at-Arms will please remove—

Hon. Members: No, no.

Mr Speaker: —Mr Baird, the Rev. William Beattie, Mr James Craig, Mr Harvey, Mr Hutchinson, Professor Lindsay, Mr McQuade, Mr Millar, Rev. Dr Paisley and Mr Poots using whatever force is necessary.

At this point Professor Lindsay (South Antrim) mounted the table and took a microphone in his hand; the Rev. William Beattie (South Antrim) removed the mace from the table and handed it to Mr James Craig (North Antrim) who carried it to the Back Bench.

Professor Lindsay: This has gone far enough.

Mr Speaker: I ask—

Professor Lindsay: This farce has gone far enough. The mace is gone. Is it OK?

Mr Speaker: I call upon—

Mr Hutchinson (Armagh) lifted a carafe of water from the table.

Professor Lindsay: No throwing of water. Have a drink yourself. We have driven the money-changers from the Temple. The mace is up. The mace is up.

Mr Speaker: Order, order. I suspend the sitting for fifteen minutes to enable members I have named to be removed.

Sitting suspended at 2.34 p.m.

Four minutes to the first suspension and the proceedings were interrupted another four times that first afternoon. Altogether eighteen loyalist politicians were carried out of the chamber by policemen. The police were on hand because the scenes were predictable. During the previous month when the composition of the Executive was known some loyalist members had been involved in wrestling and fist fights with Faulkner Unionists within the debating chamber.

Notwithstanding the dignified bearing of members of the Executive and its supporters, the loyalists were succeeding in tarnishing the image of the assembly by making it the object of ridicule. They impaired its function further by operating a partial boycott.

The impact of this behaviour was bad enough in Northern Ireland but in the rest of the United Kingdom it raised questions about the validity and viability of this devolved government. Later that year, when the infant desperately needed the supportive hand of the mother at Westminster, it was to be spurned.

TWO

After the initial fracas the dust settled. The Executive and assembly began to operate and even enjoy something of a short political honeymoon. New ministers eased into their ministerial offices at Stormont, some more effortlessly than others. Men like Faulkner had long experience in government. Unionists, even those without any such experience, found taking up the reins of power relatively painless.

But for Gerry Fitt and other SDLP ministers it was a political event and a personal achievement of considerable impact. These men had entered the political arena in Northern Ireland with an expectation of always being in opposition. This expectation was shared by the Stormont civil service and other agencies with whom the SDLP ministers would have to work, though in fairness individual civil servants, particularly those in senior positions, were conscious of the need for a new attitude to counteract the influence of half a century working with a Unionist Party.

Nevertheless there was always a niggling doubt in the minds of SDLP ministers. How much could they depend on the confidentiality of their departmental civil servants? Time was needed to build a trusting relationship.

The passage of time helped the Executive for the moment. The partial boycott by the loyalist politicians of the UUUC was being undermined in a largely unforeseen manner. The assembly had been elected under a system of proportional representation. This meant that each of the twelve constituencies had between five and eight assembly representatives from different parties. When loyalist assemblymen were refusing to raise constituency concerns in the assembly, their constituents often went to another constituency representative who would attend to their needs.

So with time, not only was the UUUC boycott coming under pressure, but the Executive appeared to be functioning efficiently. This worried anti-power-sharing loyalists like Andy Tyrie, supreme commander of the the Ulster Defence Association

(UDA), the foremost loyalist paramilitary organisation. Tyrie was to be a central figure in the UWC strike against the Executive and he had no love for SDLP politicians like John Hume, Minister of Commerce, and Austin Currie, Minister for Housing. However he recognised that both men were effective ministers, 'a damn sight better than the old farmers the Unionists put up for fifty years,' as he said to me at the time.

So for Andy Tyrie and the many who thought like him, good government in this particular instance was bad government. The loyalists believed that the long-term result of power sharing in Northern Ireland would be a united Ireland; if the Executive proved to be competent in administrative matters, so attracting more powers and increasing trust from Dublin, then the case for Protestant separatism would be undermined. Paradoxically therefore, the better this government performed, the more infuriated the large alienated loyalist section of the governed became.

Notwithstanding the vital and central role played by Tyrie and the UDA in the events of May 1974, neither the UDA or any other Protestant paramilitary organisation played a part in the Ulster Workers' Council, the flimsy cloak behind which the real nature of the strike was hidden.

The UWC appeared out of the wreckage of the defunct Loyalist Association of Workers (LAW). LAW had come into being in 1971 led by Billy Hull, who, like Harry Murray, was a shipyard union official. LAW had strong links with the UDA and both organisations suffered loss of prestige and authority as a result of the failure of the loyalist strike of February 1973. Billy Hull stood in the assembly elections but failed to be elected. LAW withered.

In November 1973 a Shorts aircraft factory worker and one-time member of LAW, Hugh Petrie, together with an official of the Vanguard Unionists, began to extend feelers to contacts in the power stations, grain mills and engineering works, mostly though not exclusively in the Belfast area. Their proposal was the formation of a new Protestant workers' organisation.

Hardly surprisingly given the record of low achievement by LAW, the response was not initially encouraging but the climate began to change in autumn 1973 after the announcement of agreement in principle to the formation of the power-sharing Executive and, even worse in loyalist eyes, a Council of Ireland.

By the time of this announcement a highly secret meeting had already taken place in Vanguard headquarters in Hawthornden

Road, east Belfast in the latter part of November. It was chaired by Vanguard assemblyman, Captain Austin Ardill. The important people at that meeting were Hugh Petrie and a group of workers from certain key industries.

Among this group was 53-year-old Harry Murray from the Belfast shipyard. Murray had been invited for a number of reasons: he was a quiet unassuming man, popular and respected in the shipyard. More important, unlike Petrie, he had not joined LAW and was not associated with its paramilitary and political connections. In the task Petrie and Vanguard had set themselves, a man with an unblemished record could be a great advantage.

Those present were unanimous in their call for yet another strike for a political purpose. However, right at the outset Harry Murray made plain his opposition to any connection with either political parties or paramilitary organisations. He viewed the involvement of Vanguard at the meeting with suspicion and stated openly that the parties were trying to fashion an instrument to manipulate the workers. Murray was never to lose his distrust of politicians. His attitude provoked heated argument and at one point he was ready to withdraw, but Petrie navigated with some skill and proposed that Murray become chairman of the yet unnamed group. He was elected.

In the few weeks up to the end of 1973 the new worker organisation put its constitutional framework together. There was to be no alignment with any political party. Each of the six counties of Northern Ireland and the city of Belfast was to elect three representatives to form a central committee of twenty-one members. The central committee would meet in each county on rota and each county was to be responsible for its own finances so that no large amount of money would accumulate in a single place.

In December the first meeting outside Belfast was held in the Seagoe Hotel at Portadown. No politicians were present. In fact, not many people turned up.

'People didn't seem too interested,' Murray said afterwards. 'There were eight people present in the Seagoe Hotel. Someone proposed Mr Paisley be the spokesman for the organisation (still nameless), but I knocked that on the head because I wanted it to be a worker.'

However, it was impossible to keep politicians out once a date for a strike had been chosen—and one was chosen. The loyalist strike was to begin on 8 February 1974.

The next meeting of the worker organisation was in a hotel in Cookstown, Co. Tyrone to prepare for the big day. On this occasion the three main loyalist politicians were present: Harry West (Official Unionist), the Rev. Ian Paisley (DUP) and William Craig (Vanguard Unionist). There were nine other people. At last they decided on a name: the Ulster Workers' Council.

If the strike had been left in the hands of this small band it would never have happened. The workers were split among themselves and the loyalist party leaders were distinctly unhappy. They knew that the UWC was not substantial enough to fill the places on its own central committee and in such circumstances organising a general strike across all industrial sectors seemed ludicrous.

The only evidence of groundwork by the UWC lay in the presence of power workers at these meetings. One of the most influential was Billy Kelly, a union official from Belfast and a founder member of the UWC. Kelly believed that a reduction of sixty per cent in electricity supply to the province would be sufficient to bring the majority of industrial concerns to a halt.

This tactic worried Murray on two counts. He did not believe that the reduction of electricity in itself would be enough to halt industry; he did not believe that the factories would stop to allow the available electricity to be diverted to other uses. Murray was concerned for the well-being of old people and babies in incubators, particularly in the month of February.

The politicians tended to share Murray's misgivings and, when this unease was added to their other basic worries about the UWC, they were prompted to vote for the postponement of the strike until 28 February 1974. They were not to know that 28 February would shake the new Executive very severely and the UWC would not be involved.

****

February 28 was announced as general election day for the whole of the United Kingdom.

Naturally the UWC cancelled whatever plans it had managed to make. The loyalist politicians were delighted. They regarded the general election as a God-sent opportunity to show their political strength in the wake of Sunningdale and the power-sharing Executive. Now they were ready for political battle under

15

their slogan, 'Dublin is just a Sunningdale away.' By contrast, the parties of the Executive were in an awkward position. They had all nailed their colours to the mast but the ship had had no time to go anywhere or show its paces.

The calling of a UK election had no connection with events in Northern Ireland. The Conservative government under Edward Heath was in conflict with the coal miners over the issue of pay restraint. It had become a battle of wills in national terms, but it scarcely received a mention in Northern Ireland, where the loyalists took control of the agenda. It was to be about republicans in government at Stormont and the Council of Ireland. Of the two themes, the Council of Ireland was the more potent. An all-Ireland institution was anathema to a large section of the Protestant vote and no amount of agreement or explanation could alter the fact.

As widely predicted at the time, the election results of 28 February were a disaster for the Executive parties. Of the twelve Northern Ireland seats in the Westminster parliament, the UUUC loyalist coalition won eleven. Only Gerry Fitt, the Deputy Chief Executive, held a seat for the pro-Sunningdale viewpoint. The UUUC claimed over half the total votes cast and trumpeted that the Executive did not have the confidence of the majority of the people in Northern Ireland.

Even though the general election result had no effect upon the majority within the Northern Ireland assembly supporting the Executive, it nevertheless was a considerable blow to the Executive and there was little it could say or do to hide the fact.

The election brought the Labour Party to power in the United Kingdom and the figures in Northern Ireland privately dismayed it. While there was a bipartisan policy in place towards Northern Ireland by the Labour and Conservative parties, the Sunningdale agreement had been a Conservative initiative. The new Northern Ireland Secretary, Merlyn Rees, was confronted with a situation not of his party's making, with an assembly which had lost dignity and now, more importantly, a Stormont administration with damaged authority.

Merlyn Rees had several courses of action open to him. He could have accepted the UUUC interpretation of the results, an interpretation shared by many uncommitted observers, that the Sunningdale arrangement did not have sufficient political support to survive the next assembly election. Under the provisions of the Northern Ireland Constitution Act 1973, which set up the assembly and Executive, the Secretary of State for Northern Ireland could recommend the dissolution of the assembly if the Executive lost the support of the electorate. But while the evidence pointed to this, the Executive continued to have majority support in its own elected assembly.

Rees could have sought the dissolution of the assembly on the grounds of public interest. This would have led to an election to the assembly and probable defeat for the Executive parties. The Executive would have fallen and direct rule from Westminster re-established.

Direct rule had always been a last resort for any government in London. Westminster neither relished nor fully understood the politics of Northern Ireland and always sought to keep them at arms length. If for no other reason, a devolved Northern Ireland government would be kept in place as long as practically possible. There was therefore no pressure from London upon Merlyn Rees to drop the Executive. Quite the contrary. He was encouraged to nurse it for a while and see what happened. Sometimes the politics of doing nothing is as viable as doing something.

Naturally the prognosis for the Executive was bleak. In spite of all the speeches of the February election campaign, in spite of Brian Faulkner's good access to newspapers and broadcasting, in spite of the reassurances of the Secretary of State, the majority of Protestants and Unionists wanted nothing to do with a Council of Ireland. The sophisticated checks and balances within the proposed council were never understood at large.

This was now recognised by sections of Faulkner's party and loyalty to the full provisions of the Sunningdale agreement began to waver. Some of them began thinking of ways to ditch the Council of Ireland. But the Council of Ireland represented the SDLP's aspiration to eventual Irish unity. Impasse.

THREE

The UWC had surfaced just before the general election polling day to speak to Merlyn Rees, who was then shadow Northern Ireland Secretary. Harry Murray and UWC treasurer, Harry Patterson, were among those who told Rees that they would bring the province to a halt unless the Executive and the Sunningdale agreement were removed. The fact that the miners in Great Britain had succeeded in reducing electricity supplies sufficiently to force industry down to a three-day working week, and through that an election, gave the delegation added faith in the use of electricity as a political weapon. It was the UWC's first meeting with the man they were to confront three months later. Rees told them that the bi-partisan policy would not be changed.

The UWC was pregnant with threat but was having trouble with its dates. From 28 February the stoppage date was moved to 8 March, and then to 14 March. Billy Kelly, the power worker, was becoming angry with Murray because of the repeated delays and there was a heated exchange between the two men at a meeting in the Park Avenue Hotel in Belfast. Relations were almost at breaking point and Kelly considered going ahead himself using electricity as the sole weapon. He had convinced UUUC politicians by this time that he could have done it, but in the end he was unwilling to proceed without full backing. The spectre of the 1973 strike was always in the background.

Murray's problem was one he never really solved but he believed he had to overcome it before any stoppage could begin. As he put it to me at the time:

I still felt we weren't ready and I had to take a lot of abuse because we weren't ready. In Belfast I had prevented any publicity about the UWC. Some people were trying to keep LAW going. We didn't want to publicise that there was another organisation superseding it. We hadn't got agents in the shipyard and in the different factories to spread the word. I wanted a little more publicity now on the organisation and its aims. I also wanted to get oil involved. I reckoned it was more important than electricity.

That last point was interesting and not one Billy Kelly would have warmed to. Murray felt that he had the right to nominate the day, especially since he was paying the bills for the initial UWC meetings out of funds from a collection he was running in the Belfast shipyard.

In Belfast the harbour estate enclosed several miles along the southern part of Belfast Lough and River Lagan. Within it lay the Harland and Wolff shipyard, which at the time was the largest single employer in the province; also the Shorts aircraft factory, another big employer—along with an airfield, some military installations, Belfast's gas manufacturing plant and an oil refinery. Murray was a shop steward in the shipyard and it was from there he set off one day in the middle of March to 'organise oil', as he put it. Note that oil had not been 'organised' for a strike even though several dates for a strike had passed by this time. The extraordinary manner in which Murray put various pieces together is illustrated in his description of that day.

> I started at the top of the road and I ended up four miles down the road, walking. I had just taken it into my head to go. I was on my knees, way past the Musgrave yard and the oil wharf. I didn't know what reception I would get but I happened to meet two blokes and I started talking to them. I got them to come along to a meeting at the Hawthornden Road headquarters a week before the stoppage.

Revolutions happen in odd ways.

Part of the credit for instilling the idea in Murray's mind must go to the Provisional IRA, who earlier in the year had hijacked a naphtha tanker on its way from the refinery to the gasworks in Londonderry. The tanker drivers retaliated by refusing to go to the city until the IRA promised them free passage. In the meantime Londonderry's diminishing gas supplies caused widespread concern and Murray logged this in his mind until the day of his four-mile walk.

* *

There was more coherent movement among the Protestant paramilitary organisations. Every Wednesday night during April 1974, meetings were being held of up to thirty men representing all the paramilitary organisations on the Protestant side. The man who convened these meetings was Glen Barr, who was to become the chairman of the committee guiding the UWC stoppage. He was one of the new men thrown up by the Protestant body politic. Young, neatly groomed, energetic, plausible and fluent; one of the very few politicians who had managed to survive in politics while retaining a well-publicised connection with a paramilitary organisation, in this case the UDA.

The Wednesday night meetings consisted of men from the UDA (Ulster Defence Association, the largest organisation), UVF (Ulster Volunteer Force), OV (Orange Volunteers), USCA (Ulster Special Constabulary Association), Red Hand Commando, UVSC (Ulster Volunteer Service Corps), DOW (Down Orange Welfare) and at later meetings, USC (Ulster Service Corps) which was found in Fermanagh and south Tyrone. The purpose of the meetings was to establish some form of political wing because it was known from experience that paramilitary candidates normally fared badly at the polls without one.

At first the gatherings were indistinguishable from meetings of the Ulster Army Council, the 'high command' of the Protestant paramilitaries. However, they found it necessary to involve people who had political advice and skills to offer. This process had begun by the end of April.

Coincidentally, the political parties of the loyalist coalition, the UUUC, met at Portrush on 26 April to hammer out a combined policy document. They decided on a platform which included the continuation of a parliament for Northern Ireland within the United Kingdom, a more intensive offensive against the IRA based on locally recruited security forces and immediate elections to the assembly at Stormont. But interestingly, they shelved a decision on a general strike against Sunningdale. Back in Belfast, the Protestant paramilitaries used this document as the basis for their first political deliberations.

Andy Tyrie, as commander of the UDA, was another of the key men at the centre of the stoppage. His plump unathletic appearance topped by glasses and a moustache disguised the ruthlessness and singlemindedness required to rise to the top of a large paramilitary organisation like the UDA, whose membership at the time was estimated at about 6,000.

When Tyrie took over the position he reorganised by centralising control to a much greater degree and imposing tighter discipline. When he had accomplished this, he investigated the possibility of breathing new life into LAW because this organisation was effectively an arm of the UDA. The two shared the same offices. However, he faced two major difficulties. The first was that LAW would need rebuilding from the ground up, and secondly he knew that another Protestant worker organisation, destined to be the UWC, was beginning to emerge. In these circumstances he judged it would be easier to establish paramilitary influence in the new worker body.

Tyrie believed the loyalist politicians, Paisley, Craig and West, to be rivals in this endeavour and that, unless he did something about it, the new workers' body would succumb to the influence of politicians. In his own words:

> The politicians always detested not being able to control LAW, so behind closed doors they tried to start another workers' organisation. They got in touch with certain people and invited them to their meetings, saying that if they were going to take over Northern Ireland they'd need to control certain things. So they got these men together, which flattered them, and decided on this workers' council.

This was Tyrie's interpretation of the beginnings of the UWC and it probably led him to over-estimate the influence of the loyalist politicians within the UWC. However, the politicians were supporting Murray's caution about a starting date, saying that they would need to prepare the ground first. Also in the background was the fact that Tyrie had been angry with Craig ever since the February 1973 strike. Tyrie had understood Craig to have blamed the UDA for the debacle, saying that the UDA did not have the capability of backing a strike, a euphemism for frightening people from the workplace.

Nevertheless Tyrie was a practical man and was backing Craig and the other loyalist leaders in seeking a delay in starting the strike.

****

The meeting which finally decided the date for the stoppage took place at the beginning of May in the UDA headquarters in the Shankill area of Belfast. It was not a UWC decision.

Tyrie was aware of the vacillation about dates and was sufficiently annoyed to tell the UWC group that their strike was not taking place until he said it could. He was also annoyed to discover that the worker organisation he aspired to take over was scarcely worth the trouble. Like Murray, Tyrie did not believe that cutting off electricity would in itself be sufficient to bring down the Executive. He believed, correctly, that the workforces of most other industries had not been prepared for a strike.

It is a matter of conjecture whether Murray ever admitted to himself the logic of his position, which was that if he wanted a general strike he would be the prisoner of the paramilitaries because most workers would not leave the factories unless they were frightened away, or locked out because electrical supplies had been withdrawn completely.

Both groups, workers and paramilitaries, believed the loyalist politicians of the UUUC were powerless and therefore did not invite them to the Shankill meeting. The paramilitaries invited the UWC people under the pretext of healing the rift with the rump of LAW. Tyrie had told Murray that if they were all going into battle then all differences should be healed in advance. Murray agreed and made sure that the members of the Belfast County Committee (in reality, the only part of the UWC that existed) turned up. When they arrived that night they could recognise only one member of LAW.

'Where are the phantoms?' Murray asked mockingly.

Only then did it dawn upon him what the real purpose of the meeting might be. The men in that room represented every Protestant paramilitary grouping and their aim was to pin the workers to a definite course of action so that the paramilitaries could be ready on the day.

Kelly was delighted at this turn of events but the paramilitaries were worried about the timing. Glen Barr was chairing the meeting and he was recommending that the strike call must be linked to an event. The strike needed a starting gun of some kind, if the metaphor is not too graphic. One suggestion was that the strike begin on the morning of 14 May to coincide with the continuation of a debate about the Sunningdale agreement in the assembly. Barr modified this to the vote at the end of the debate.

The loyalists were bound to lose and a sense of defeat could be the trigger.

Andy Tyrie still thought that decision was wrong and this remained his view even after the strike had been successful. Tyrie had been a shop floor worker in a Belfast foundry and knew something about industrial action.

If you want to reduce opposition to a minimum, then begin your strike on a Monday when people generally don't want to go to work. I wanted the intention to strike declared after the assembly vote and the strike proper to begin the following Monday. This would have given us the rest of the week to get our propaganda going, to have electricity reduced enough to stop the factories even beginning to turn and altogether would have encouraged more workers not to go in of their own accord.

Tyrie foresaw that a midweek start to the stoppage was going to give the UDA and other paramilitaries a lot of extra work.

But even at this late stage Murray was half thinking of delaying action once more and gave this account of an exchange between himself and Billy Kelly, the electricity worker.

Murray said to Kelly, 'What is the next date we could go on from a power station point of view, because the light is becoming too bright? It's just about right for me now because people wouldn't be in too much darkness from long nights.'

'You will not be able to go until October or November,' Kelly replied.

'That's all I want to know.' Kelly had finally convinced Murray it was now or never. The paramilitaries were as happy as they ever would be and the attitude of the UUUC politicians was of little importance to him. There was just one question left. Would the assembly actually move to a vote on 14 May? It was within its powers to carry the debate over another day.

* *

The Saturday before the stoppage the UWC met in the Vanguard Unionist headquarters at Hawthornden Road, which was in a pleasant middle-class residential part of Belfast, not far from Parliament Buildings at Stormont. This house was to become a well-known landmark as the headquarters of the UWC during the strike.

There were about a dozen people present including, as Murray put it, 'Two old gentlemen from Omagh. I didn't know their names and they didn't represent anyone but they came to all the meetings. They carried messages back to a small association or a Vanguard-type organisation.'

The Ulster Workers' Council was a grand title for a very small and informal ad hoc committee.

The topic under discussion that Saturday evening was the public's evident lack of interest in plans for a strike. Few people believed such plans were serious and so it was decided that Murray, the press officer Jim Smyth and Billy Kelly should go over to the BBC studios in Belfast. Their aim was to create panic by advising housewives to store up food because there were going to be massive shortages and a power shutdown.

The journalists in the BBC newsroom refused to listen to the relatively unknown group which suddenly and unannounced turned up on the doorstep promising chaos. The three men left threatening that when the stoppage happened, the BBC would receive no co-operation from the UWC.

But the BBC was not the only quarter to disparage the strike call. On the evening before, Harry Patterson, Harry Murray and Hugh Petrie met a few of the loyalist politicians in a hotel in the loyalist stronghold of Larne. The Rev. Ian Paisley, John Taylor and Ernest Baird then learnt the full extent of what was being planned. It differed from the token stoppages politicians had in mind and they opposed the plan.

At the time John Laird, a senior member of Harry West's Unionists, said, 'We still felt we hadn't pulled out all the political stops. On the other hand we were politicians with responsibility and no power and any politician who gets into that position is a twit.'

****

It was 14 May. The politicians and the stoppage leaders met again at Stormont. The UWC's Bob Pagels, Murray and Patterson arrived to watch the Sunningdale debate and to see if a vote was taken at the end of the day.

At issue was a motion proposed by John Laird on behalf of the loyalist assemblymen. It read: 'That this assembly is of the opinion that the decision of the electorate of Northern Ireland at the polls on 28 February 1974 rejecting the Sunningdale agreement and the imposed constitutional settlement, requires re-negotiation of the constitutional arrangements and calls accordingly for such re-negotiation.'

According to parliamentary practice, it is possible to propose an amendment which negates the original purpose and intention, so Brian Faulkner on behalf of the majority who supported the Executive, proposed this amendment:

That this assembly welcome the declaration by the Executive that the successful implementation of its policy depends upon the delivery, in the letter and spirit, of commitments entered into by the British and Irish governments; calls upon those governments to fulfil such commitments; and expresses confidence that if these commitments are fulfilled, the system of broadly based government established under the Northern Ireland Constitution Act 1973 will enjoy the support of an overwhelming majority in the parliaments of the United Kingdom and of the people of Northern Ireland.

The first main speaker was the deputy leader of the Vanguard Unionists, Ernest Baird. He outlined the threat. 'I have talked to some of these people, including Mr Harry Murray and Mr Billy Kelly, and I understand that they are saying that if those who are supporting this Executive—the Faulkner Unionists—persist in voting against the will of the people as expressed through the ballot box they will have no alternative but to bring industry to a halt.' He went on,

. . . they have explained the situation in so far as a layman like myself can understand the intricacies of the power game in the sense of electricity. At the moment some 725 megawatts of electricity are going out all the time to the province. That is sufficient to keep going industry, essential services, the farmers and the housewives. About two-thirds of that electricity is used by what one might describe as the farming community, the hospitals, the drainage services and the housewives. Only one-third or less than a third is used in industry. That may be surprising but it is a fact. As I understand it, in the initial stages the men will be cutting down the power output to some 400 megawatts. That will give cuts all over the country but it is up to the Minister of Commerce to decide how this electricity is to be used.

I want to assure this House that if there are [power] cuts leading to hardship in homes or to old people or in hospitals or any other essential service, it will not be the responsibility of the power workers. The responsibility will lie entirely on the shoulders of the head of the Department of Commerce, Mr John Hume.

The ploy of convoluted logic can work. By the end of the strike a large proportion of Protestants were blaming the Executive for the damage.

Baird's speech was an attempt to paper over the cracks between the position of the loyalist politicians and the UWC, cracks that were widening even as he was on his feet. Murray, Patterson and Pagels were watching from the public gallery even though they had not intended to. They left to try to find a cup of tea and ended up in the loyalist party rooms, where a heated exchange of views ensued.

Murray recalled the episode.

Most of the prominent loyalist politicians were there. Big Ian [Paisley] was on the telephone to the police about his security guard because it had just been taken from him. And Bill Craig, whose house had just been bombed, had lost his security guard. This is what was in their minds. It was typical of them. The three of us were worried they seemed to have no will to win. We told them they were bankrupt of ideas and were finished as far as leading the people was concerned. I said the people were leaderless and none of them knew which way to turn.

I was greatly distressed to hear Craig say in that room that we wouldn't last twelve hours, that we would not get support. Bob [Pagels] was very hostile. They didn't seem to care and we walked out of the room.

The row damaged their morale. If the strike did indeed fail, the loyalist politicians would not protect them. Privately the politicians were opposing them. Murray was depressed.

The roof could have fallen in on me. I turned to Craig and asked if there was anything they could do. He said there was not and that the strike would be a failure. I looked all around at them—Ardill, Baird, Craig and Paisley—and none of them would even make a move with his lips. It was coming up to ten to six and Paisley wanted West to carry on [speaking in the debating chamber] over the time so that there would be no vote that day. This would mean a fortnight or three weeks before another vote. When he [Paisley] put that to me I told him it wasn't on. It was now or never.

But an account from a politician who was present states that the three UWC men were under pressure that afternoon and at about half past five they panicked. He said the workers were the men who wanted the debate continued because they were not ready. It was the politicians who said that the die had been cast and that UWC men would have to be satisfied with whatever had been arranged for the stoppage.

Just before six o'clock the Northern Ireland assembly divided for the first time in its short history, and as it would transpire, its only time. The loyalists lost by twenty-eight votes to forty-four. In a corridor a BBC journalist found Harry Murray alone and told him the news of the vote, pressing him to come to a nearby television studio. Murray wanted to have Bob Pagels and Harry Patterson confirm the figures but the television programme was on air and could not wait. He had to decide himself.

He turned and went into the studio.

****

On the morning of Wednesday 15 May the response to the strike call was poor. An overwhelming majority of the workforce turned up for work.

'It wasn't organised,' Harry Murray said afterwards. 'The people weren't educated.' Murray thought his own wife was joking that morning when she asked him why he was not at work. Nor did Bob Pagels' wife take him seriously, at least not until she went into the kitchen of her Belfast home to make breakfast to find there was no electricity. She thought a fuse had blown. When the truth dawned she felt the same as most. 'What on earth are we striking for? Do we need all this?'

At Stormont the stoppage was not foremost in the minds of the Executive. Its members were pleased to have reached the end of the Sunningdale debate the previous evening. For weeks the vote had been delayed by what amounted to a filibuster by the UUUC parties and the debates had been dreary and repetitive. For the UUUC there had been advantage in having the loyalist viewpoint reported in newspapers, radio and television at some length. The Executive regarded the end of the debate as the passing of an obstacle rather than the approach of one and paid as little attention to the strike call as the rest of the province.

The Harland and Wolff shipyard was a good indicator of what was happening within the Protestant urban communities. On the first morning of the stoppage a very large number was at work—this at the very place where Harry Murray was a shop steward. The problem was not simply a lack of enthusiasm; many workers were plainly opposed to the stoppage.

Support for the stoppage in the shipyard was largely confined to a couple of hundred stagers in the shipyard. These were the men who erected scaffolding or staging round a ship under construction and as a group had the reputation of being hardliners. A meeting was called for ten o'clock in the morning at the head of the large building dock. Consistent with the feeling in the yard it was sparsely attended and adjourned as a flop. The organisers called another meeting for lunchtime but this time the stagers went round the buildings and plants drumming up support and there was a larger attendance at the second meeting. Those against the strike did not have much opportunity to vote against it. The motion put to the workers was whether or not they were against the Sunningdale agreement and in a mainly Protestant workforce the outcome was predictable. 'That's it. You're out,' said the platform.

There were some ineffective protests at this from the floor before the meeting broke up. The workers were still slow to leave the shipyard but were hastened on their way by rumours that the shipyard was the only large concern still working, or that workers' cars still parked in the yard after a certain time would be burnt or that paramilitaries were already putting up barricades cutting men off from their homes. Small wonder that the bulk of the workforce left after lunch, though some held out and were still at work at half past three that afternoon.

One such man was Sandy Scott, the chief shop steward, who was very much against the stoppage at the beginning, though, like so many others, he was to change his mind in the light of Northern Ireland Office attitudes. It had crossed his mind to try to counter what was going on.

I didn't go to the meeting at lunchtime because I realised that the muscle boys were going to put the pressure on. I've no doubt that the general feeling inside was against the strike but I knew that back in the ghettos it would be a different matter. They would give way under pressure. The barricades would go up and they would not be able to get out.

That is precisely what happened.

Bob Pagels had at least organised within the animal feedstuff mill in which he worked and only a few men turned up for work on Wednesday morning. In common with much of Northern Ireland the mill management was confused. Pagels was supposed to be at work at six o'clock in the morning. At seven the mill management telephoned him to find out what was happening and he went down to the mill to explain. On the way he saw cars parked round one of Belfast's big engineering works, Sirocco, and wondered why. This was the plant where the Jim McIlwaine, secretary of the Belfast County UWC, worked. Surely it could not be working—but quite evidently it was. Pagels entered and met a nonplussed Jim McIlwaine wearing his non-working good clothes who told him that the Sirocco workers did not want to strike.

'I must have a wee talk with them,' Pagels said. 'They'll have to fall into line.' Pagels went onto the shop floor, wearing a coat and a pair of sunglasses. He walked through the lines of machines shaking his fist. The image was enough. Large numbers of workers left soon after.

In microcosm, that was the story of the first few days, a story of massive intimidation. The most effective shutdown was in the port of Larne, a ferry terminal about twenty-three miles from Belfast. Larne was very largely Protestant and from the beginning was controlled by Protestant paramilitaries. Nearly every business in the town closed on the first day; men in combat jackets carrying clubs ensured that shops shut; the harbour area was sealed off with a barricade of two cars and a container lorry. In fact, Larne was shut down so tightly that some of the organisers of the stoppage at the Hawthornden Road headquarters were complaining about the inconvenience.

Larne was an important port but it also controlled the approach to the biggest power station feeding the Northern Ireland grid. The situation in Larne therefore gave the paramilitaries an independent capacity to reduce electricity supplies without reference to the UWC power workers or their leader, Billy Kelly.

Later in the day the police cleared the barricade blocking the single road to the port but by that time British Rail, which operated the route to Stranraer in Scotland, had cancelled the service until further notice. The early morning ferry which had already left Scotland was ordered back to Stranraer.

Meanwhile other big factories outside Belfast were coming to a halt. At the ICI fibre plant near Carrickfergus, halfway between Larne and Belfast, 1,500 men walked out. This was the first blow to the man-made fibre industry which was well established in the province. The sector was more sensitive than most to labour trouble or power failure because the plants involved a continuous process. They needed to be kept running or be shut down in a controlled fashion to prevent molten plastic gumming up the works. In other towns, such as Portadown which like Carrick-fergus and Larne had a majority Protestant population, the strike began to take hold. The way the stoppage began was much the same. Workers turned up because nothing had been organised to the contrary. A mass meeting was then held called by activists for the purpose of supporting the Protestant cause. At this point the dividing line between intimidation and legitimate communal pressure becomes difficult to draw.

The UWC was a failure right from the outset. It had failed to establish even an elementary form of framework for something as ambitious as a general strike and therefore never had a chance of convincing and persuading workers to strike. The UWC's only success was in the power stations where the levels of electrical supply were reduced to sixty per cent by lunch-time on the first day. However, workers sent home from the factories because there was no power or because they were frightened were involved in a lock-out, not a strike.

The UWC was prepared to gamble on a mass lock-out based on the withdrawal first of electricity, then oil. Harry Murray was explicit when he talked to the paramilitaries at the Shankill Road meeting shortly before the stoppage began. He had said, 'It's either civil war or passive resistance, pulling electricity and petrol right down, if the response on the second night had not been what it was. I didn't care who went to work. We were determined, the four of us.'

The four of us.

The paramilitaries saw through the UWC claims. Glen Barr and Andy Tyrie did not believe that the UWC had enough strength to organise in the power stations and at one point told Billy Kelly and his colleague, Jack Scott, that their claims to have planned in the power stations for eighteen months was a load of rubbish (putting it politely).

Strangely the paramilitaries were more sensitive to the need for political considerations to be taken into account. The less preparation, the more the paramilitaries would need to intimidate, but the lesson of the February 1973 strike had been learnt by the paramilitaries in greater depth than by the UWC activists. Immediately before the strike Andy Tyrie gathered the brigade staff of the UDA and told them that the workers had no idea of how little support they had. 'It's going to be up to us to do the dirty work again,' he told them. 'But we are going to have to make sure there is no violence this time. If there is any violence then everybody is going to back away.'

Non-violence is not a prominent characteristic of paramilitary organisations and Tyrie had to argue his case long and hard. (It should be noted that, in the UDA, intimidation was held to be non-violence.) He said that if they did not bring about the downfall of the Executive on this occasion, the failure would put the loyalists back four years, which was how long Tyrie believed it would take to regain the confidence of the ordinary Protestant. It might be worse, he had said, for at the end of four years the loyalists might have already lost. A failed strike would bolster the Executive.

This meeting of UDA leaders was important. When the 'brigadiers' agreed on a strategy and showed themselves capable of carrying it out, this had a bearing on the response by the army, the police and the politicians in power.

In Tyrie's view intimidation (he called it 'discouragement') had to succeed in the first few days of the stoppage. So the UDA, the UVF and other members of the Ulster Army Council mounted their campaign to close factories from lunchtime on Wednesday, when they issued a statement ordering all loyalists to cease work forthwith. An Army Council statement read, 'Ulster Army Council personnel and pickets will receive directives to permit essential services to persist. These will be given over the communications media. All other movement will cease.'

This action continued on Thursday and Friday, by which time they considered the job almost finished. Note the assumption that the directives could be relied upon to be passed on by the media, a subject which I will return to.

But the statement had another effect. It demolished the fiction that the stoppage was a spontaneous or planned worker action. It demonstrated that the UWC had become the creature of the Protestant paramilitaries. The UWC men and representatives of the paramilitaries met publicly at the Hawthornden Road head-quarters for the first time as a co-ordinating committee. It was a large and cumbrous body of sixty which proved so unwieldy that a small 15-man committee was set up after the first weekend.

FOUR

The attitude of the political establishment to the strike call and related events particularly during the opening days puzzled many people. On the Tuesday night when the strike had been declared, the House of Commons at Westminster passed an order legalising Sinn Féin, the political arm of the IRA, and also the loyalist Ulster Volunteer Force. The UVF was to play a major part in intimidation during the next few days and was an important member of the Ulster Army Council. The UDA had always been legal.

The timing was a coincidence. The new Northern Ireland Secretary of State had told the Commons a month before of his intentions, explaining that the people of Northern Ireland had to be encouraged towards political activity. The move was carried out in the face of implacable hostility from Brian Faulkner and the Executive. However, real political power did not lie with the Executive but with people like Merlyn Rees and his Minister of State, Stanley Orme, whose offices were in Stormont Castle, adjacent to the Executive offices in Parliament Buildings at Stormont.

On the day Westminster passed the order, Brian Faulkner's opposition was being widely reported in the newspapers. Speaking at a debate in Sheffield University, he attacked the IRA as the principal enemy while at the same time declaring he was in no way soft on Protestant violence.

> It causes me particular distress when I see members of my own community descending to crime and violence. The hideous sectarian killings are a shame and a disgrace to any Christian community. I condemn them utterly. I hate the whole rotten gamut of paramilitary organisations and this is why I believe it to be wrong to legalise the activities of the UVF and of Provisional Sinn Féin.

Such feelings underlay Faulkner's initial reaction not to negotiate with the UWC because he saw, correctly, that the force of the stoppage at the beginning was the Ulster Army Council. However, later he was unable to divine the watershed point when a majority of Protestants changed their minds and began supporting the stoppage.

Meanwhile propaganda began in earnest. The UWC announced that power would be produced for households and essential services but would not be available if John Hume 'squandered it' on industry. In other words, the Executive was being invited to close down industry even though there might be enough power in the grid to keep it going. John Hume's Department of Commerce replied speedily to say that it would be impossible to maintain all domestic supplies if electricity reduction made cuts necessary.

At the end of the first full day most factories and shops were shut and, although the effect was magnified by half-day closing in Belfast and some surrounding towns, it was evident that the strike organisers had been successful, notwithstanding the means used. Merlyn Rees was in London. In his absence, Stanley Orme decided to meet the loyalist political leaders and members of the UWC at Stormont Castle that evening.

William Craig, John Laird and the Rev. Ian Paisley saw Orme first. They explained that the stoppage was not what they wanted but they understood the reasons behind it. The politicians had been thinking of other ideas. Some of these had already been partially operated by Protestants, such as a boycott of goods made in the Republic of Ireland, such as not accepting Irish currency which at the time had sterling parity and circulated freely in Northern Ireland. Some had suggested sabotaging the system of Giro bank payments as operated by the Post Office. However, the ideas had not fired the imaginations of Protestants and the politicians had lost the initiative.

That Wednesday evening Stanley Orme may have believed that the politicians wielded influence with the UWC and paramilitaries since he did not know of the altercations that had taken place between the groups in the run-up to the strike. Orme had a number of things to get off his chest. He warned the politicians that the strike could have serious repercussions on public opinion in the rest of the United Kingdom. The UUUC politicians were already suspicious of public opinion on the other side of the water and Orme's words cut little ice. As they spoke, Harry West, leader of the Official Unionists, was in London addressing the right-wing

Monday Club, urging greater constitutional separation between Great Britain and Northern Ireland for protection against what he called 'the crude ignorance and wrecking from Westminster'. Members of the Monday Club must have wondered why such people were calling themselves loyalists as he continued:

> We hope that this decadent period in British politics, which has been so disastrous for us in Ulster, is only a passing interlude. But we would like to be armed in some way against a recurrence of it. When one has had experience of dealing with people whose word has not proved to be their bond, one wants a bond as well as words.

So the disillusionment was mutual, and Orme's words were falling upon deaf ears back at the Castle. However, the most unproductive part of the evening had yet to come. While the politicians were with Orme, Murray, Patterson and Pagels were waiting in the car park below. With them were Andy Tyrie and Tommy Lyttle of the UDA and Ken Gibson of the UVF (next to the UDA in importance in the Ulster Army Council). Except for Billy Kelly from the power stations, that car park contained the men behind the stoppage. They had been waiting for almost an hour, their mood becoming darker with the passing of each minute. Eventually Tyrie exploded in a cascade of expletives and said he was not waiting any longer, but before he could leave the door of Stormont Castle opened to admit them.

Once inside the first problem was introductions. It was explained that the representatives of the paramilitaries were present only as observers. Orme did not wish to be seen talking to paramilitaries. To get round the difficulty of the UDA having two observers, Lyttle was introduced as a member of the Orange Volunteers. This did not fool the civil servants present, but nobody made an issue of it. A civil servant asked Tyrie quietly to explain to him who everybody was but since the paramilitaries had had only a short acquaintance with the workers, Tyrie was embarrassed when he could not remember Bob Pagels' name or where he worked.

The meeting was counter-productive from the outset. The following impressions were what the group left with and helped shape the co-ordinating committee's intransigence from this point on. Murray told me:

Orme started off with a tirade of abuse. He called me a bigot. He said if we didn't call off the strike the troops would grind us into the ground. He said we had no chance of winning and he would not give in. There was a lot of arguing going on. Bob had his dark glasses on. The three of us gave him a go about the civil rights campaign. He marched and led the civil right campaign in Derry and slept in John Hume's house for a fortnight. . . . He was a committed man, a United Irishman.

And from Bob Pagels: 'I went on about security. He was telling us about the great job the soldiers were going to do. I asked him if he thought of the soldiers when they were getting shot . . . he blew up and waved his arms about.'

In the shambles the permanent under-secretary at the Northern Ireland Office, Frank Cooper, found himself the subject of one digression bordering on farce. 'Frank Cooper was sitting beside Orme whispering in his ear,' Murray went on. 'I kept staring at this man who was behind Orme's back nodding "no" all the time we spoke. I said to him, "Stanley, see your mate there. You'd better tell him to stop shaking his head because it's going to fall on the floor and I don't want to pick it up."'

But there were some genuine debating points made. Murray said: 'Your leader Harold Wilson said that Ted Heath put us in the Common Market and that it was to be renegotiated, Rees said that were are not having an [assembly] election for four years. Seeing we're all British and we all believe in British democracy, I would ask that Sunningdale be renegotiated.' Orme replied, 'You're a bit of a comedian, aren't you?'

There could be no meeting of minds on the constitutional question. That much was clear. Electricity became the topic towards the end of the meeting and the central concern of the delegation was the Maydown industrial complex outside Londonderry. Maydown's workforce was largely Catholic and not therefore answering the call to down tools. Nor was it being intimidated. Also at Maydown was the Coolkeeragh power station. Protestant pickets were infuriated because the only way to close Maydown was by closing down Coolkeeragh, not possible because half the power workers there were Catholic.

The delegation demanded that Maydown, with its eighty per cent Catholic workforce, be closed. Orme pounced on the sectarian nature of the demand. The delegation said that because

Maydown was using power, Protestant areas of Londonderry, including a bakery, were being left without power.

The point the delegation was trying to make was that the sixty per cent of power being produced was for essential services (as defined by themselves), not industrial complexes. When the meeting broke up some of the delegation thought somehow that an understanding had been reached with the government to the effect that if the power went no lower than sixty per cent, then government would put pressure on big complex like Maydown to close.

Tyrie, who simply listened as an observer, remembered the UWC men saying that they would hold power at sixty per cent providing government shut down factories, including Maydown but he did not recall any specific reply from Orme. When later the UWC said that there had been an agreement, the government strenuously denied it. It is difficult to see how Orme could have made any such commitment; it would have been totally inconsistent with the Northern Ireland Office policy adopted throughout the strike. The only reference to an agreement by a loyalist politician was made by the Rev. Ian Paisley who had complained at the meeting that some workers were being locked out of their power stations. If this continued, he had said, then all labour would be withdrawn from the generators. When there was still electricity the next morning it was presumed that agreement had been reached not to lock out any power workers.

When Orme spoke to journalists on the steps of Stormont Castle after the meeting he made no mention of any agreement. He said that there had been some straight talking and, perhaps a little euphemistically, that there had been a detailed discussion of the political situation, including Sunningdale and political power sharing.

Orme had taken an uncompromising line and, remembering the February 1973 strike, it was a perfectly valid initial response to sit back and wait for the backlash against widespread intimidation, or for violence and a backlash against that. The tide of condemnation which had swamped the 1973 strike seemed to be swelling once more and with it the hopes of those supporting the Executive.

Pro-Executive politicians began their offensive. Brian Faulkner said that the public was again being made the target of irresponsible extremists who were abusing the freedom of the press and television to make the most reckless pronouncements without regard for the consequences. Where did these people come from, he demanded? What was their authority?

However, a statement by Faulkner's own party was not quite as thunderous. It tried to explain away the assembly vote which supposedly had triggered the UWC strike. It was not, the party statement said, a vote in favour of signing the Sunningdale agreement. Strictly speaking this was correct but it sounded less than a battle cry, more like a plea for mercy. Individual members of the party were more positive, men like Peter McLachlan, a member for South Antrim, who said, 'We stand absolutely firm for our British tradition while extending a hand of friendship to the Irish tradition and are determined to remove the violence and the scars of violence from the face of Ulster.'

The Presbyterian Church was the largest Protestant church in Northern Ireland. Its government committee passed a resolution condemning 'the inevitable intimidation involved in political strikes on the part of any section of the community'. It said the strike would further damage relations between Protestants and Catholics and bring hardship and loss to everyone.

The chairman of the Northern Ireland Confederation of Shipbuilding and Engineering Unions, Andy Barr, appealed to trade unionists to stop and think and return to work. He said opinions about the constitutional framework differed widely within the confederation and that therefore the correct means of applying pressure was through the assembly at Stormont. He was particularly angry at the intimidation, and like many others, could rattle off a list of firms which had suffered threats.

As a Labour politician, Stanley Orme placed significant value on the condemnation of the strike by the trade union movement in Northern Ireland. His wide trade union experience in the rest of the United Kingdom led him to expect that solid trade union hostility would undermine unofficial action in the end. As a newcomer to the province, he did not seem aware that parts of the trade union leadership in Belfast, while effective in matters of pay and conditions, were divorced from the majority of rank-and-file Protestant members in their political standpoint. This lack of knowledge led to a humiliating defeat for the government later in the strike.

In the meantime morale in the Northern Ireland Office and within the Executive remained high as they waited with some confidence for cracks in the loyalist ranks. Already one loyalist politician, William Thompson of West's Official Unionists, had declared himself absolutely opposed to the strike. He said that attempts at political change, no matter how essential or desirable, ought to at all times to be carried out through normal political channels.

He perceived that once groups with industrial or military power begin wielding extensive political power, then the politician is left without a role. By contributing support to extra-parliamentary action, as did important loyalist politicians, they demolished much of their own authority. During the stoppage loyalist political leaders were leaders only in name; true political power lay with the paramilitary organisations.

The fact that the stoppage was successful in loyalist terms did little to release the politicians from their invidious position. Behind the lip service to them afterwards was a strong vein of contempt.

FIVE

On Thursday 16 May the strike bit deeper even though electricity was maintained at sixty per cent of normal. Engineering was the hardest hit sector. Harland and Wolff with over 10,000 employees lay idle, as did the Sirocco engineering works and the Shorts aircraft factory.

Some tried to continue working. At Mackies, a large engineering works on the Springfield Road in Belfast, approximately a quarter of the employees turned up but fled when a group of men entered and ordered them out. Petrol bombs were reported being thrown into the Gallaher factory car park in Belfast. Notwithstanding Tyrie's efforts to keep violence at a minimum, intimidation in places was very rough and very crude.

A 25-year-old engineer was pulled from his car at two successive barricades and badly beaten up. He spent the night in hospital. More people were hurt outside the Michelin plant at Mallusk when pickets fought with day-shift workers coming out of the factory. Many of the victims were women since the men had largely stayed away. The men had been told their cars would be burnt. Other factories in south Antrim halted as the campaign of intimidation intensified. Standard Telephones and Cables and ICI with 5,000 workers between them ran down their production, as did the Carreras cigarette factory and the Courtaulds fibre plant.

The Engineering Employers Association received complaints about intimidation all day but nobody seemed to be able to stop it. Altogether 40,000 engineering workers were out.

A bogus car bomb was used to stop the Metal Box plant in Portadown. A car hijacked in the largely Protestant Edgarstown estate was abandoned outside the factory. Several industries in a new industrial estate outside Portadown closed after visits by groups of men, and many of the town's pubs remained closed.

The extent of intimidation decreased in areas where the proportion of Protestants in the population diminished. So west of the River Bann which divides the province north to south, intimidation was less evident. In Strabane, for example, a predominantly Catholic town, employees reached places of work without trouble, but all too often found themselves without work because there was no electricity. Similarly in Omagh, the county town of Tyrone, where the creamery and milk processing plant was particularly badly hit. The firm stopped accepting tanker deliveries of milk and found itself facing a long queue of farmers with churns of milk. But the plant could not operate without electricity, and forward planning was impossible in the face of unpredictable power cuts.

The stoppage demonstrated that farming was very dependent upon electricity. Intensive farming was particularly demanding on power. By the second day of the stoppage the Ulster Farmers Union was drawing attention to the growing plight of egg, pig, poultry and milk producers. The Milk Marketing Board, to which all farmers were required to sell their milk, was attempting to allay fears about doorstep milk delivery but its general manager said he could not guarantee the service if the stoppage continued. However, milk delivery was already in difficulty. The dairies did not have enough power to sterilise bottles and the milkmen were being intimidated off the streets. In some cases milk floats were hijacked to form barricades and the milk was stolen. It mattered little that milk was on the list of essential services as defined by the UWC.

The full UWC list of essential services was as follows: bakeries, groceries, dairies, chemists, butchers, confectioners, electricity, gas, water, sewage, hospitals, animal feedstuffs, farmers, wages, banks, schools, medical services, hospital transport, school transport, solicitors, newspapers, normal recreational activities, coal supplies and postal services. The original list did not include postal services until it was discovered that postmen were the people who delivered the benefit Giro cheques.

The inclusion of animal feedstuffs in the list did not stop several animal feed trucks ending up on the barricades. Another favourite among all barricade builders was the corporation bus. After a dozen had been hijacked, Citybus withdrew all services at eight o'clock in the morning of Thursday 16 May.

A large number of vehicles were hijacked because hijacking was a mainstay of the intimidation campaign. There was a deliberate policy not to burn them, as had often happened in the past. However, neither the UDA nor the UVF could keep control of excited crowds and there was rioting in east Belfast. On the

Ormeau Road shots were fired as police were removing a hijacked lorry blocking a bridge and in the same area police scattered a crowd trying to batter down the door of a pub. In the afternoon of Thursday 16 May there was an ominous outbreak of sectarian rioting in the New Lodge area of Belfast where Protestant and Catholic communities interfaced. Troops broke it up. This type of violence had become less prevalent in the years up to 1974 but an upsurge was half expected as the stoppage progressed.

For the first time Protestant action was seriously interfering with schools at the time of examinations. Hundreds of children were absent, including many who should have been sitting papers for the Certificate of Secondary Education (CSE). Absenteeism was highest in the Protestant areas where roadblocks had been set up. The senior education officer for Belfast joined the growing list of those who were discovering that classification by the UWC as an essential service was meaningless. School transport was impossible in some areas.

On the evening of Thursday 16 May the UWC decided on the unusual step of closing all pubs, hotel bars and drinking clubs. This was the result of pressure from the wives of men who were not at work. A group of women stormed into Shankill Road pubs declaring that if their husbands were losing money in a strike, they should not be spending what little they had on drink. Pubs, they shouted, were emphatically not on the UWC list of essential services. The counter argument that pints were 'a normal recreational activity' did not prevail. One man who had been chased from his pub on the Shankill by a crowd of women with umbrellas and bags of flour, stormed straight into a ladies' hairdresser establishment and chased the women out. One woman said that her hair was only half done. The man said that his abandoned pint was only half finished.

Harry Murray, like Brian Faulkner, was teetotal. The drinkers had no friend at the top in either camp and swathes of Protestant drinking came to a halt for the remainder of the stoppage. Bars in Catholic areas did a roaring trade.

An unforeseen repercussion of the stoppage was a big reduction in the weekly payments made by the UDA and the UVF to the families of loyalist prisoners held in the Maze and other prisons. The main sources of these funds were the drinking clubs run by paramilitaries.

****

On the morning of 16 May the Northern Ireland Economic Council met at Stormont under the chairmanship of Faulkner. Accompanying him was the head of the Department of Commerce, John Hume. The Council was a joint body of leading industrialists and trade unionists. Predictably, it took a grim view of the strike with a statement that also directed veiled criticism at the Northern Ireland Office, which retained the responsibility for security:

> To remain on strike, or to prevent others who wish to go to work from doing so by blatant intimidation, is to level a great blow at confidence from which the interests of the whole community will suffer in time to come. The Council is also convinced that the authorities have a duty to take steps to enable those wishing to go to work to do so, for example, by removing barricades.

By ten thirty that morning it was clear to the Council that the paramilitary organisations were preventing people from going to work or forcing them to leave work if they had already done so.

Both Faulkner and Hume gave their full support to the inclusion of the sentence about removing barricades as a message to Rees and Orme. If the Executive had had some responsibility for security the history of this fortnight might have been very different. Faulkner was a very angry man. He had been forced to travel to his own office by helicopter by the security authorities because the roads were not open. During the flight, he saw the barricades for himself and hardly needed to read the flood of reports about road blockages and intimidation on arrival.

Faulkner immediately complained bitterly to Rees who told him that the army and police had been instructed to take down all the barricades. He told Faulkner that the picture he was painting was inaccurate! Containing himself, Faulkner told him that there was a barricade blocking the entrance to Dundonald House, the main civil service office block within the Stormont estate. Rees did not believe him and sent someone down the hill to find out. (The Secretary of State can live and work in Stormont Castle without setting a foot outside.) The messenger returned and confirmed not only the Dundonald House barricade, but that there was another one not far away.

The episode worried Faulkner because there could be only two explanations for Rees's behaviour. Either the man did not know the full extent of the breakdown of normal law and order, or that he did, had ordered counter-measures and had been ignored. Either situation was cause for anxiety.

However, throughout that day, the first Thursday, the police had been removing barricades in Belfast. The city got its buses back. Nonetheless, the crucial time for keeping the roads clear, as Faulkner knew, was early in the morning when people were trying to get to work. This had not been done. It was of little use having roads open at midday. By that time the workforce was resigned to staying at home.

Throughout the first three days of the stoppage, Faulkner, his deputy, Gerry Fitt, and the rest of the Executive tried to get the Northern Ireland Office to act by deploying a large number of troops as a show of force. Andy Tyrie and Glen Barr, who chaired the strike co-ordinating committee, agreed in the immediate aftermath that if the troops had swamped the streets at the outset, diluting the most obvious intimidation, the outcome could have been very different. Tyrie said the UDA had been under strict orders not to engage the army because the experience of the 1973 strike had shown how counter-productive this could be.

There is some evidence that the army was dragging its heels.

After the strike was over, an article appeared in a magazine of the club whose members Harry West had addressed on Tuesday. The club said it had been submitted under a pseudonym because the author was a serving officer. In it he wrote:

> The unwillingness of the army to act to bring about the end of the strike (on the quite reasonable grounds that there was little or nothing it could do within the concept of minimum force) and the subsequent confrontation between the military and the politicians, must be the most significant event of recent years. For the first time the army decided it was right and the politicians had better toe the line. The consequences of this are yet to be fully appreciated.

Many members of the former Executive believe that this article stated the truth. According to many of them, the army's reluctance to act stemmed from the belief of the General Officer Commanding Northern Ireland, Sir Frank King, and other senior officers, that an operation to break down all the barricades would need to be massive and might provoke a strong military reaction from the Protestants.

The extent of the barricaded areas gave military intelligence a good idea of the numbers in paramilitary organisations and a good assessment of the support for them among ordinary people. In the last resort, the army would rather not risk starting a shooting war with Protestants while trying to deal with the IRA. At least one Executive member remembered that every time the idea of increased army action was raised, Rees talked about armed reaction by the Protestants. Certainly at the beginning of the strike, Rees and Orme believed that the full use of the army was an option open to them. That is what they told the UWC delegation in Stormont Castle.

On the afternoon of that first Thursday, both Rees and Orme were in the Commons at Westminster for Northern Ireland Question Time. Captain Lawrence Orr, South Down, was stating the loyalist case. 'If the government proceeds with a policy of endorsing Sunningdale, completely repugnant to the majority of Ulster people, it is the government who are responsible for the havoc at present being wrought in Northern Ireland.'

In his reply Rees referred to the army. 'You and your colleagues will soon have to face up to the fact as to whether your loyalism will lead you to come up against British troops.' Did loyalism mean getting one's way—or else? Or did it mean they wanted to be part of the United Kingdom?

If loyalists were squaring up to British troops, there were those in Great Britain who saw precious little difference between loyalist and republican resistance. Some were becoming restive at the amount of money the Ulster situation was costing. Orme told the Commons that in the first four months of the year, claims for £10.5 million had been received for damage to property. A Labour MP said that the average British family subsidised the Northern Ireland economy to the tune of £30 per annum. All this was meant as a warning to the strike leaders but it went unheeded. The Prime Minister was listening, even if no one in the province was.

* *

Amazing though it may seem, the Executive at Stormont did not give the stoppage its undivided attention during those crucial first few days. In its defence one can point to the widely held view at the time that lack of support evidenced by the amount of intimidation necessary would inevitably bring about a collapse. Even the loyalist politicians had not come out in public support. That did not happen until the fifth day.

So the Executive was in step with a large body of reasonable opinion in refusing to take the strike too seriously. There were other reasons. At that time, the Executive was contending with two other problems which threatened its cohesion. A deep rift had developed over the Sunningdale agreement between the two biggest Executive parties, the Faulkner Unionists and the SDLP. The Faulkner Unionists were seeking modification of the Sunningdale agreement in the light of the 28 February election result. The other problem centred on a 25p 'fine' on public authority housing tenants who had been on a rent and rates strike for over a year in protest at detention without trial or internment.

The 25p problem came to a head first. Though it was unlikely to bring down the Executive, it was capable of inflicting a nasty wound. The SDLP had been partly responsible for the rent and rates strike in the first place as a political weapon before power sharing became a possibility. It was an alternative confrontation strategy to that of the IRA, in the eyes of the SDLP. Now that the SDLP was in government, Catholic pressure against the government was no longer appropriate, but how was the SDLP to get off the hook?

It was decided to impose a financial penalty on anyone still withholding their rent after a certain date. At the beginning of April 1974 Austin Currie, Minister for Housing, announced in the assembly that a 25p per week collection charge, together with an increase in the amount which could be deducted at source from social security benefit to pay the rent, would be introduced on Monday 20 May. The SDLP was not very happy with the decision. The party was committed to securing an end to internment without trial and the number of releases since they had taken office had been disappointingly small. It was therefore arranged on that day in April when the announcement was made, that an SDLP backbencher should ask a question to allow Currie to add a qualification. The qualification was that if all British commitments to the SDLP were not honoured by 20 May, then the party would reconsider its decision in the light of that. In other words, the civil disobedience would be called off if the British government began phasing out internment, as it had promised.

It was a difficult position for the SDLP—being a party in government in Northern Ireland but being in opposition to the British government on certain issues on the nationalist agenda. Currie felt that in the circumstances the SDLP had to do something about the rent and rates strike; he was sensitive to Protestant anger over its continuation. But on Friday 17 May, the last working day before Monday 20 May, the deadline, Currie entered the Executive meeting and proposed that the measures aimed against the rent strike should be postponed.

There was an immediate row with the Unionists. Currie had been forced to retreat from his original position by opposition within his own party, not least because by then there were more people interned than when the party had taken office. Currie rationalised his position by arguing that he was talking people out of the non-payment campaign at the rate of a thousand a week and that the introduction of a 'fine' would be a wrong reaction.

This position was not accepted by the Unionists. Roy Bradford, Minister for the Environment, and Herbert Kirk, Minister of Finance, led the Unionist attack saying that such last-minute reversal would damage the credibility of the Executive. Furthermore in a situation where the Unionists were in a tight corner, being accused of conceding too much at Sunningdale, a surrender on the 25p fine would have been to attract yet more criticism. They thought it obtuse of the SDLP even to suggest the idea when the loyalists outside were tightening the screw.

In the back of Currie's mind was something else. He thought that the loyalists themselves would go for a rent and rates strike either as part of, or alongside, the stoppage. Looking ahead, he saw the trap awaiting an SDLP Executive member who shrank from action against Catholic tenants. Such a member would have been stripped of the moral authority to deal in a similar way with Protestant non-payers. What was being demanded of Austin Currie, the party politician, was diametrically opposed to what was being demanded from Austin Currie, the government politician.

The compromise he sought was postponement rather than revocation of the order but this was dismissed out of hand by the Unionists on the Executive. Herbert Kirk as Minister of Finance had signed the original order six weeks before. He was making it plain that his signature cancelling the order would not be forthcoming.

The last card Currie could play was to threaten resignation and this had as little effect as his other cards. One other member also threatened to resign. Paddy Devlin was the SDLP Minister for Health and Social Services and it was he who would have the responsibility of deducting the 25p from the benefit of non-payers. He himself lived in a rented public authority house in Belfast in a Catholic housing estate where the rent and rates strike had been very strong. Very awkward.

Paddy Devlin saw himself being manoeuvred into being Austin Currie's debt collector, something he would be loath to do even for his best friend. The two men disliked each other.

Fitt, the SDLP leader and MP for West Belfast, had been over to London the previous day for the Westminster debate and arrived back on Friday's midday plane. He was therefore late for the Executive meeting.

Rees and Orme were attending the meeting, though it was unusual for them to do so. However, the circumstances of the loyalist strike were demanding concerted and combined Executive and Northern Ireland Office consideration. As Fitt breezed in, exuding his almost permanent air of optimism, he was met with the kind of situation no party leader ever wants to experience. Frank Cooper, the permanent under-secretary at the Northern Ireland Office, intercepted him to say that Devlin was resigning from the Executive.

Sure enough, there was Paddy Devlin laboriously writing out his resignation in longhand, watched by the rest of the Executive, the Secretary of State and the Minister of State. Over his shoulder could be read:

My attitude on this matter has been made known to a limited range of people since the issue arose. I have remained patient in the hope that the written commitment we received on a number of occasions by your predecessor in government would be honoured by you. Instead I find you have promised to bring into being a small committee of five people to assist with the re-settling problems of released detainees and you have done nothing else towards that commitment.

Against that I received weekly reports of mass assaults by military in detainee compounds; the female population detained in Armagh Prison is doubled; the number of people detained in Long Kesh is increasing daily; assassinations of isolated members of the minority soar to the deafening silence of your inertia, and six weeks ago you announced at Westminster without consulting the SDLP, that you intend to reactivate the Emergency Provisions Act 1973, though we in the SDLP had been given to understand by Francis Pym, the Secretary of State last December, that the opposite course of action would be followed.

I have been told on two occasions that large-scale releases were to take place on the week the Westminster elections were announced. Based on that, one could conclude that the arrangement for releases had already been set up. These releases were never put into effect. The responsibility is yours entirely. You have had ample time to produce proof of your determination to end detention.

I am now of the opinion that this issue, which is one of our prior reservations when taking office in the power-sharing Executive, is not to be met. Thus I am faced with a personal decision regarding my position on the Executive.

In view of my belief that you are not seriously intending to honour this commitment in these circumstances, I could not participate in the imposition of penalties on householders suffering from the same misgivings on the end of internment as I myself share.

The only honourable course is to withdraw from the Executive and I request you to recognise this letter as my resignation.

He sent the letter out to be typed and told Rees that his resignation would be effective from six o'clock the following morning, Saturday 18 May. There was an air of gloom. A resignation on any issue at the beginning of the loyalist strike was a grave blow. For the SDLP it raised the problem of finding someone to take Devlin's place and this was going to require an explanation to the rank-and-file as to why the other SDLP members of the Executive had not resigned over the internment issue. The party leaders did not regard that as an insuperable problem, just a messy one.

Among the SDLP leadership Devlin was seen as being out on a limb. Some of his colleagues believed he had been looking for a way out of the Executive because of the problems being in government had been causing him and his family in his volatile constituency. It is clear that the rest of the SDLP ministers did not regard the 25p issue as one worth resignation. But Devlin was close to the grass roots of nationalist opinion and the resignation spelt trouble.

But behind the scenes was an even bigger row on the horizon: the watering-down of Sunningdale. Devlin, a hardliner, would have made compromise even more difficult than it undoubtedly was going to be. To that limited extent there was relief that he was leaving this particular stage.

Suddenly the door opened and a piece of paper was handed to Faulkner at the head of the table. Faulkner looked shaken, then read it out.

Dublin had suffered multiple car-bomb explosions. Thirty people had been killed.

It was the worst single outrage to date in the still small years of violence. In the circumstances Devlin froze his resignation.

SIX

In point of fact car bombs had exploded in two places over the border in the Republic, Dublin and Monaghan.

The three cars containing bombs in Dublin were stolen in Belfast. A green Hillman Avenger which exploded in Parnell Street was hijacked by two armed men in the loyalist Oldpark area. The driver had been blindfolded and taken to a house where he was kept until three in the afternoon. The driver of a green Austin 1800 which exploded in South Leinster Street told a similar story. He too had been hijacked in loyalist Agnes Street, off the Shankill Road, and then kept prisoner in his own house in Torrens Road until three o'clock. The third vehicle, a blue Ford Escort, was stolen from Duncrue Street some time between eight and eleven o'clock in the morning. It detonated in Talbot Street in Dublin.

All three bombs in the Irish capital exploded without warning at approximately five thirty in the afternoon, in the middle of rush hour. The result was carnage. Blood literally ran down the gutters. Twenty-two people died immediately, others later and 134 were injured. A complete family was wiped out when a young couple with two baby girls aged five months and eighteen months were walking past the Ford Escort. It was only when the mutilated bodies of the babies had not been claimed by the next morning that the authorities realised that what remained of their parents was in the mortuary as well.

In a Portadown car park a green Hillman Minx was stolen between three thirty and four in the afternoon. It was packed with explosives and driven over the border to Monaghan where it exploded just after a quarter to seven, killing another five and injuring fourteen. Again no warning was given.

The effect of the bombs on strike-bound Belfast was electric. Some thought that the strike was being revealed as the beginning of outright civil war in Ireland. Immediate IRA retaliation was expected. Catholic areas were alive with rumours that the Protestants were poised for attack on them and there were reports that both the Provisional and Official wings of the IRA were preparing to hand out arms.

Bombing by Protestant paramilitaries in the Republic was not new. It was a tactic used intermittently along the border. The targets were normally public houses, garages and filling stations, though occasionally they had attacked the centre of towns. But the bombs of 17 May were of a different order of magnitude and viciousness from what had gone before. They had required effort from at least perhaps twenty people belonging to an organisation based in Belfast and Portadown. Suspicion fell on the two biggest Protestant paramilitaries, the UDA and the UVF.

After the stoppage was over, something of myth took root that the two-week period of the strike had been relatively peaceful, that when the might of the Protestant people was mobilised there was no terrorism stalking the streets. The carnage in Dublin drew most of the attention. The following day's bombing in Lisburn (Co. Antrim) letter boxes went comparatively unnoticed even though flying debris injured several Saturday shoppers and a policeman.

According to the myth, the UWC strike made it virtually impossible for the IRA to operate, but this was untrue. On the first full day of the stoppage, two members of the Official IRA were shot dead in an unoccupied farmhouse near Newry while preparing a mine. On the same day two soldiers were shot and wounded in separate incidents in Belfast and Londonderry. On the day of the bombings in the Republic, a man and woman booked into a room in a hotel in Rostrevor, Co. Down and planted a ten-pound bomb. Warnings were telephoned and nobody was hurt. In Armagh high velocity shots were fired at an army post. In Dungannon a large bomb in a culvert under a road was defused. In Londonderry an army mobile patrol came under fire and booby trap bombing. In other incidents in Belfast a man was badly beaten up, civilians were shot at from cars, two men were shot in the leg and shots were heard in various parts of the city.

All this in the first few days of the strike. The province was not at peace nor anywhere near it.

****

On Tuesday 14 May, the day of the Stormont debate on Sunningdale, Glen Barr and another loyalist assemblyman colleague, Hugh Smyth, were at the Maze prison visiting loyalist prisoners. They had wanted to be at the debate but Smyth had been unable to arrange the visit for any other day. When the two men had finished at the Maze they drove to Stormont in the hope that the debate might still be in progress but arrived too late and everyone had gone.

Barr left Smyth and went to the home of the UDA commander. He and Tyrie discussed what had happened and what had to be done over the next few days because no full meeting of the co-ordinating committee had been arranged until Friday. They decided not to put up barricades or start the process of 'discouragement' until the extent of the workers' organisation—or lack of it—became clear.

When as they suspected, voluntary support was low, the UDA and other paramilitaries swung into action without reference to the UWC people, still less the loyalist politicians. Barr then left Belfast for his home in Londonderry where he remained until 17 May. He set off for the co-ordinating meeting on that day in his car.

He was nearly killed.

While he was on a long straight stretch of the road near Toome on the shores of Lough Neagh, his front-wheel-drive Renault 16 broke a drive shaft while travelling at about seventy-five miles an hour. The remains of the shaft sliced through hydraulic brake lines. When Barr discovered in the next instant that he had no brakes, he automatically attempted to use engine braking, but since the engine was no longer properly connected to the driving wheels, nothing happened. The handbrake was ineffective. In desperation, he mounted the grass verge and rough ground slowed the car over a distance of a few hundred yards.

If this had happened on anything but straight road, Barr's role in the stoppage might very well have ended with his own stoppage.

He was given a lift by a friend whose car he had passed at high speed a little earlier and arrived in time to chair a meeting of the large co-ordinating committee at Hawthornden Road in Belfast. Barr's Derry home was not far from the Maydown industrial estate and he was able to see for himself that it was functioning. Maydown was indeed continuing as best it could with the available electricity supplies.

An incident in one of the Maydown plants illustrated the dilemma of factory managements during the stoppage. Hutchinson Yarns had been running their plant and this was evident to workers at the nearby Coolkeeragh power station. Coolkeeragh was one of the two big power stations of the generating system, capable of supplying 360 megawatts from its oil-fired boilers and alternators. This was equivalent to approximately half the requirements of the province in early summer—a fact which later became central in a dispute between Hume as Minister responsible for power, and the Northern Ireland Electricity Service.

The electricity service was walking a tightrope by trying to produce as much current as possible without provoking a reaction from the Protestant power workers, who were trying to keep electricity to sixty per cent of normal. By Thursday 16 May the power workers had been told, incorrectly, that an agreement had been reached between the UWC and the Northern Ireland Office to shut down big industrial complexes if electricity was not allowed below sixty per cent. (This was the supposed agreement from the meeting between the UWC and Stanley Orme on the Wednesday evening.) So the Protestant workers at Coolkeeragh were now threatening revolt because Hutchinson Yarns was working using their electricity.

The electricity service wanted to start up another boiler and alternator, known as a set, to add another 120 megawatts for peak loading. The men refused to do so until Hutchinson's closed. An approach was made to the plant but Hutchinson management refused to bow to this kind of pressure and was supported in its stand by the Department of Commerce.

After three hours talking the position of each side was unchanged so the new set was not brought into play. Therefore the supplies failed and Hutchinson Yarns closed. Principle if little else was satisfied on all sides. Hutchinson's would have closed anyway because of pressure from within the works and the whole oil-fired section of Coolkeeragh shut down later that day when the UWC decided to reduce supplies still further. From this time, 16 May to the end of the stoppage, the only electricity produced from Coolkeeragh came from a small gas turbine unit producing only 60 megawatts. Also on the same day, the workers shut down the coal-fired part of the main station at Ballylumford at Larne. These closedowns reduced the generating capacity by a total of 480 megawatts at a time when normal consumption would have been 750 megawatts.

The following day, Friday 17 May, the electricity service thought that the collapse of the system was inevitable when workers in the two Belfast power stations walked out. Belfast East produced 120 megawatts and Belfast West 240 megawatts, both from coal. The workers in these stations had heard that a connector link over the border with the Republic of Ireland's grid was being used to supply power to Northern Ireland. Electricity service management quickly pointed out that the link had been cut by an explosion on 8 February and had not been repaired. The link, when it was operational, ran from Tandragee in Co. Armagh to Louth in the Republic and was capable of carrying 300 megawatts in either direction. It was established to share spare generating capacity in the two systems. Unfortunately it ran through south Armagh, a stronghold of the Provisional IRA. Unwittingly by severing the link the IRA had may have helped its enemies, although it was established practice in normal times not to use the link as a means of nullifying industrial action in either system.

When the Belfast power workers were satisfied that the link was down, they went back to work. The electricity service stated that without the contribution from these two stations, the system could not operate. This was not true, however, because three days later the men did walk out. While this caused headaches for the distribution engineers as we will see, a solution that kept some power in the grid was found. The electricity service was not being deliberately untruthful; the situation was unprecedented and the waters were uncharted.

In the meantime rota cuts were causing general dislocation. The Northern Ireland Hospitals Authority warned the workers not to bring about a complete shutdown because lives would be put in danger. The authority pointed out that while hospitals could cope with power cuts, life support systems could not continue for very long on hospital emergency generators. Some treatment such as radio therapy had already been reduced because it needed high and constant voltage.

By Friday petrol supplies had begun to dry up even though the stoppage organisers were not by then directly targeting this fuel. Some of the big oil and petrol marketing companies withdrew their road tankers completely on Thursday 16 May. As a result some filling stations were running out and customers were being limited to a pound's worth of petrol. As motorists became aware of this they began to hoard.

The electricity cuts were imposing a form of rationing anyway since the pumps would not operate without power. A few enterprising garages kept their pumps going by jacking up the driving wheels of cars and running a belt drive to the pumps. This worked until the petrol ran out.

Meanwhile the effect of the strike on the farming community was becoming ever more severe. Thousands of gallons of milk were being poured down the drains of farms. Meat processing plants and abattoirs could not slaughter and freeze. Eggs and bacon, two important exports, could not reach their markets.

Poultry farmers were not receiving enough electricity to keep their broilers alive and they warned of the wholesale slaughter of hens, which was to happen the following week. The president of the Ulster Farmers' Union, Joe McCahon, pleaded with the UWC to alter its policy. 'There will be a shortage of food in the shops,' he said. Like so many others, he complained that being on the UWC list of essential services was of little significance at street level.

Whether or not McCahon realised it, the threat to food supplies was exactly what the UWC wanted. It had tried unsuccessfully to have the BBC transmit warnings about shortage of food the Saturday before the strike. Panic about food could only rebound on the government. As the first weekend of the stoppage approached shopkeepers experienced a run on food supplies. The Smyth and McClure chain of food supermarkets began selling off frozen food at half price. Their freezers required only a few hours of electricity per day to maintain the low temperatures but repeated warnings of the imminent shutdown of all power had had its effect.

Bread disappeared from nearly every shop within minutes of opening, as did dried milk. The public was beginning to believe that dairies and bakeries would be used as weapons. The stark truth was that there would be no essential services for the general populace, only for the Protestant paramilitaries to keep them operating. Those services would be petrol for transport and telephones for communication. Everything else would be expendable.

There were many in the opposing camp who believed that the way to beat the stoppage was to allow the full consequences of it to fall unshielded. At the beginning the Executive did consider being ruthless in this manner but the strategy was not possible for two reasons: firstly, the Executive did not have the necessary powers to carry such a policy and secondly, there was not the necessary degree of unanimity within the Executive to decide such a policy.

To some observers the policy being enacted seemed the reverse of ruthless. Paddy Devlin's Department of Social Services decided during the second week to pay unemployment benefit and other benefits without the normal checking procedures and in the first week, on 17 May, Leslie Morrell's Department of Agriculture allowed the Milk Marketing Board to pay farmers for milk not received at the creameries. Part of the reason was that farmers were forbidden to sell their milk elsewhere and milk delivered to creameries was being refused.

In spite of what Paddy Devlin was about to do himself, he was very critical of the Milk Marketing Board decision. He felt that up until that point the farmers had been putting pressure on the paramilitaries and the UWC but afterwards, when they could be paid for pouring milk into rivers, they threw their lot in with the strike. In the first few days the farmers and their union were making angry noises; by the second week cavalcades of tractors and farm machinery were appearing in support of the stoppage. However, the Department of Agriculture was caught in the same dilemma as the Health and Social Services. Both were dealing with people who were losing through no fault of their own. It meant paying for just under 2.75 million gallons of milk which had been destroyed.

The two initial days which Glen Barr had spent in Londonderry established the guiding hand of the paramilitaries and the time had come for another move on the political front. So far there was no evidence of middle ground between the opposing sides. Having said that, middle ground was difficult to delineate because the UWC was so disorganised. It had general aims; little detail in place.

For example, on the day the strike started one UWC spokesman was saying that nothing less than a new election for the assembly would suffice and another talked vaguely about 'a definite change in the political climate'. Their Wednesday meeting with Orme at Stormont Castle must have demonstrated to the UWC that the beginning of the stoppage had effected no change on the political climate, except in the wrong direction. There seemed to have been a hardening of the hostility towards the loyalist position. Another meeting had been arranged for Friday between the loyalist political leaders and the Secretary of State, who had missed the Wednesday meeting because he was in London.

On Friday afternoon Barr was chairing the co-ordinating meeting and an immediate question was what attitude to adopt to the forthcoming meeting of the politicians with Rees. Reaching consensus among the large group was not easy and it settled for a wait-and-see policy. What would Stormont offer them? However the prevailing mood was to be flexible. Interestingly, by that first Friday many in that room in Hawthornden Road thought that time was not on their side and the UWC position might be weaker in a few days time.

Rees had spent all day of that Friday at Stormont, largely dealing with the Executive and the difficulties within it. He had told the Executive that the Sunningdale agreement could not be ratified unless the SDLP and the Unionists could settle on what form the Council of Ireland should take. He had also discussed the legislation needed at Westminster to establish a common law enforcement area in Ireland as part of the Sunningdale agreement. The report of the Anglo-Irish Law Commission had been made available to the Executive three weeks earlier and its contents had disappointed the Unionists. It was to be made public in less than a week, though much of it had already been leaked.

In summary therefore, it had been and unsettling and disappointing day for Rees and Orme. There seemed to be nothing on the table that the Executive was inclined to agree about. Its members were fighting among themselves, and when Rees and Orme left the room they had been carrying the resignation of one of its members. The afternoon had finally ended with the news of the bomb massacres in Dublin and Monaghan. A thoroughly depressing day.

The Executive was still in session when William Craig, Harry West, the Rev. William Beattie (DUP) and Glen Barr (Vanguard Unionist) arrived at Stormont Castle. The Dublin bombs were exploding as they did so though none of them knew it at the time. It did not help that the two sides were approaching the meeting within different contexts. The loyalist politicians were there to suggest that they adopt the role of mediators between Stormont and the UWC. Rees believed that UWC representatives were to accompany the politicians for, as a Northern Ireland Office spokesman had put it, the Secretary of State was prepared to talk to them but not to negotiate.

The chances of negotiation seemed remote anyway after a very uncompromising statement issued by Rees that afternoon.

Those responsible for the organisation and implementation of this dangerous and coercive campaign must realise that they are acting against the interests of the people they claim to represent. They are also seeking to dictate to government. I must make it clear that there can only be one government which is responsible to all the people of the United Kingdom through Parliament at Westminster. The situation is, that if it is not possible to maintain output at the power stations, we shall be faced with a total blackout of the province. If such a situation developed, hospitals would be unable to function, lives would be lost through lack of operating theatres, food supplies would be curtailed and many other serious consequences would follow. This is the stark truth which the whole province must face.

The UWC had issued its own bleak picture. Unless the government climbed down, power would be cut off and housewives were advised to stockpile food before shortages became worse. It referred to an indefinite stoppage. Orme was accused of not passing to the electricity service the supposed undertaking to shut down industry in return for electricity being held at sixty per cent and they attacked the threatened use of troops to break the stoppage. 'If it was acceptable to the British Labour Party that the miners' strike could be used to bring about political change in Britain, then they must equally accept the rights of the Ulster workers to pursue their legitimate demands using a similar strike.'

With this kind of run-up, it was hardly surprising that the loyalist politicians left Stormont Castle after a mere forty minutes without any progress. If anything, positions had become more entrenched. Rees made it clear that he would not give way and call an early election to the assembly. Nor would he scrap the Sunningdale agreement. He told the UUUC politicians that just as the IRA had been unable to bomb its way to the conference table, so the UWC would be unable to strike its way there.

'My instructions are quite clear,' Rees said after the meeting. 'There will be no agreement with people who strike for political ends. This is the firm view of Her Majesty's government and there was no chance of it being any different.'

The Executive took some heart from words like these. In its eyes the refusal to negotiate was an expression of strength. In any negotiations there could be only one item on the agenda: the Executive itself. An election to the assembly at this time would diminish the strength of the Faulkner Unionists to the point that, were the Executive to fall, Sunningdale would go with it. British government policy was to ride out the storm.

The problem, of course, was that the government in Westminster was not directly in the firing line. The subsidiary government in Belfast was, and it needed more than fine words. There were suspicions that perhaps the hidden agenda of London was to submit Faulkner's Executive to trial by fire.

But by early Saturday morning, the fourth day of the stoppage, the Executive and its supporters were taking heart. The Protestant middle classes seemed to be against the strike; the farmers were saying they were against, the managerial classes were doing everything they could to keep factories running, the technical staff running the electricity distribution grid were stretching their meagre electricity supplies, a large number of small shopkeepers were against, and so were doctors, teachers and lawyers.

Even some of the loyalist rank-and-file politicians were unhappy. That morning a member of Craig's Vanguard Unionist Party, the Rev. Robert Bradford (who in 1981 became the first Westminster MP from Northern Ireland to be assassinated by the Provisional IRA), appealed to workers to return because he felt politicians could achieve the strike aims. He was the second UUUC politician publicly to voice opposition, William Thompson, Official Unionist assembly member, being the first.

Nevertheless these two were out of step. The rest of the UUUC felt it had no alternative but to go along with the stoppage.

Rees and Orme that Saturday morning were lodging hope on a meeting of trade unionists called by the Confederation of Ship-building and Engineering Unions and the Joint Industrial Council for the Electricity Supply Industry. Four hundred were present at a meeting which started late because of a telephoned hoax bomb. They decided on two back-to-work marches in Belfast, one to the shipyard, the other to the Castlereagh Industrial Estate in Protestant east Belfast. To head the marches they would invite the most prestigious figure in British trade unionism, Len Murray, General Secretary of the British Trade Union Congress. He had offered to help the Northern Ireland Committee of the Irish Congress of Trade Unions in countering the stoppage.

The marches were scheduled for the morning of Tuesday 21 May—a week into the strike. However, by that time the situation had changed drastically. Up until Saturday morning, the Executive and the Northern Ireland Office had seemed merely to have stood still. Those against the strike, or lock-out as many termed it, were now looking desperately to government for a lead, for positive action. It began to dawn on moderates that the Executive was powerless and rudderless. Even more alarming, so was central government at Westminster.

This was a watershed.

SEVEN

At this crucial juncture one spark of hope briefly flickered when a group of Belfast people made intensive political efforts to seek a negotiated solution. Its failure is worth recording as a revelation of why the ruling establishment behaved like a rabbits caught in headlights and squandered their support in Northern Ireland.

The Northern Ireland Labour Party (NILP) was one of the casualties of competing nationalisms and religious or cultural division in the province. The political labels of Left and Right were rarely used by commentators in discussing Northern Ireland, at least not in the sense commonly understood in Great Britain or elsewhere. The NILP was once the largest of the small steps Northern Ireland politics had made in the direction of unalloyed socialism or social democracy. The Social Democratic and Labour Party might dispute that, but this party's social democratic and labour credentials were always less important than the constitutional Irish nationalism it stood for. Nevertheless the SDLP was clearly a left-of-centre party and leftist Catholic politicians were at this point in history gathered in much greater numbers under the SDLP flag than that of the NILP, which became perforce more of a non-Catholic party of the left. It had also become a rump with a single assembly member, David Bleakley. Small and weak though it was, the NILP earns a place in the story of the stoppage.

The NILP was among those organisations and individuals which sensed early and accurately that the mood among the majority of Protestants, particularly those initially either lukewarm or against the strike, was beginning to change. Some party members began looking for a workable compromise quite early into the strike. Bleakley had tried unsuccessfully to propose a compromise motion during the debate about Sunningdale. On the first day of the strike the NILP leader, Brian Garrett, called for troops to be deployed in the power stations to forestall intimidation. His party was supporting the Executive and power sharing.

Notwithstanding the close relationship that had developed

between the SDLP and the British Labour Party, the NILP was also a sister party so the NILP had some privileged access to Stormont Castle. On the evening of Friday 17 May Garrett and Douglas McIldoon, party secretary, met Martin Reid, who was a senior official in the Northern Ireland Office. This meeting took place only two hours after the Dublin bombs and at a time when there was widespread fear of IRA retaliation in kind. The atmosphere was not conducive to the message from the NILP men. Garrett and McIldoon told Reid that Stormont should be prepared to open negotiations with the loyalists, particularly in circumstances where it appeared that the army was not to be used to its fullest extent. Reid asked how the Secretary of State could negotiate with the UWC, a self-appointed body allied to the paramilitaries. But Garrett and McIldoon insisted that Rees was impaling himself on a hook. They asked to see Orme.

Orme appeared and was clearly nonplussed that a fraternal Labour Party thought he was tackling matters the wrong way. While Orme was talking of beating the strike because no one was going to bomb their way to the conference table, the Labour men were pointing out that equating striking with bombing was ludicrous, and the Northern Ireland Office, through intransigence, was about to sacrifice the Executive.

The gap between the points of view could not be bridged. Garrett and McIldoon were convinced that time was not on the side of the Executive. They believed that trade union opposition to the strike would count for nothing. Their report back to the party stated: '. . . the strike would gain public sympathy in contra distinction to the Vanguard strike of 1973 and in that event the assembly Unionists would collapse and power sharing would be lost. On the other hand a settlement could be quickly devised acceptable to the loyalists and which would retain the essential principles of the 1973 Constitution Act.'

The following day Garrett sought a meeting with Rees for a delegation which included David Rowlands, Director of the Northern Ireland Community Relations Commission, Peter McLachlan, Faulkner Unionist assembly member, and Brian McGuigan, Chairman of the moderate New Ulster Movement. Rees refused to see them and instead they saw James Allen, a Foreign Office civil servant on attachment to the Northern Ireland Office. But the message was the unchanged; the Northern Ireland Office would not negotiate.

The following day, Sunday 19 May, McIldoon and other party members drew up a memorandum of a possible basis for settlement. They showed its contents to some members of the UWC and unofficially received a favourable response. However, it was never put to the co-ordinating committee of the strike, but at the time Garrett and McIldoon were convinced that a negotiated settlement was within the realms of possibility. The UWC seemed uncertain and divided that weekend; possibly that could have been exploited.

The wisps of agreement centred on a calling-off of the strike in return for loyalist politicians being included in the Executive and the watering-down of the Sunningdale agreement. Since even the Faulkner Unionists were beginning to push for a watered-down Sunningdale, such a proposal was not completely unrealistic, though it does not take account of the SDLP position. The NILP submitted this document to the Northern Ireland Office on Sunday 19 May, indicating that some UWC people were aware of its contents and might consider it a basis for dialogue. This is what the memorandum said:

(a) The supreme irony of the present confrontation is that it is between two adversaries—Her Majesty's Government and loyalists—who should have the same object, i.e. the inclusion of loyalist opinion within the power structure of Northern Ireland.

(b) Given this, there is no excuse for Her Majesty's Government pursuing a policy of confrontation with the loyalists and either seeking to punish the entire community or humiliating the loyalists.

(c) For even if the loyalist strike is broken, the essential political fact will remain that the task of assimilating the loyalists into the structure of government here will not only remain unaccomplished but will be even more difficult to accomplish. The chance of violence again setting the pace in loyalist politics will re-appear. Striking and bombing are not equal degrees of iniquity.

(d) We would argue that this crisis offers the Government the opportunity of forcing the pace of change in Northern Ireland by assimilating the loyalists into the system.

(e) Essential to our view therefore is an initiative from Government or the Executive to meet the strikers.

(f) We believe that over the crisis of the last year, an Ulster near-consensus had evolved. Essential to any way forward is:

> (i) the preservation of power sharing as a principle and the present constitution as a means to that end, if only on a temporary basis,
> (ii) the British connection,
> (iii) the window to the South,
> (iv) effective security measures.

A settlement might be based on the following:

1. The establishment of an all-Ulster conference as a constitutional forum to hammer out any changes that may be required in the details of the constitution but respecting the principles outlined in the following clause.
2. By acceptance of all the parties in the assembly, in the form of a solemn resolution, that the only way forward for the Ulster community is on the following basis:
   a) partnership through power sharing until such time as non-sectarian politics have evolved,
   b) that developed and cordial relations with the Irish republic are essential,
   c) that Northern Ireland's desire to remain within the United Kingdom is the only basis for peace, prosperity and stability for the foreseeable future and for as long as the majority desire it.
3. The establishment of a caretaker Executive until new elections are held—such an Executive to include representatives of the loyalist parties.
4. A commitment that the assembly will not run until 1977.
5. The establishment of inter-governmental North/South relations on the basis of equality, with diplomatic recognition of the North being implied pending any changes in the Republic's constitution.
6. The commitment that any powers according to any future all-Ireland institutions, whether in the first instance or subsequently, should be subject to a referendum in the North, thus retaining control over our own destiny.
7. The establishment of an all-Ireland Security Advisory Committee for the duration of the present IRA campaign, with membership and channels of communication from

all Dáil and assembly parties to give security advice to British and Irish governments.

8. To speed up the procedure for ending detention.
9. The establishment of a joint committee to determine means whereby parity of income with Great Britain can be assured for Northern Ireland workers.
10. The provision of money out of public funds to political parties for education purposes.
11. Request to meet the Ulster Workers' Council from the Secretary of State for Northern Ireland or the Northern Ireland Executive.

With the hindsight of almost twenty years, the document makes interesting reading. The agenda for those seeking rapprochement has changed very little; the bones of an interim Northern Ireland peace agreement lie within it.

Some of the clauses were obviously more important than others. Stripped to its essentials, it meant re-jigging the Executive and constructing another without the millstones of a full Council of Ireland and loyalist obstruction. As the White Paper produced by the Northern Ireland Office after the fall of the Executive demonstrates, and as the document itself makes plain, none of the provisions ran counter to British policy in Ireland.

Rees was perfectly willing to abandon the Executive to its fate if he felt he could construct another (and even if he felt he could not, as events seemed to show). The fly in the ointment was the SDLP. As Rees and Orme were aware, one SDLP member had very nearly resigned because of disagreement with the more flexible Faulkner Unionists. Feelings at the time were running so high that if Rees had put the document cold to the Executive for serious consideration, it would have collapsed there and then.

But in order to retain the possibility of salvaging important parts of the 1973 Northern Ireland Constitution Act such a sacrifice could be justified because in the end the Executive fell anyway, but taking everything with it. The Northern Ireland Office was unable to perceive that the NILP memorandum had wider support, well outside the confines of the party itself. In an effort to demonstrate that point, the group who had been to the Castle on Saturday spent Sunday and Monday phoning what the called 'responsible organisations', asking them to a gathering in the Quaker Meeting House in Belfast. These organisations included churches, the Northern Ireland Council of Social Services, leading members of the medical profession, prominent businessmen and trade unionists, city councillors, community workers, members of political parties and even government departments. The agenda was narrowed to finding a method of removing electricity from the battle—a device which could have provided a formula for talks. But it had become a fast-moving situation and by Tuesday evening, when the 300 delegates eventually met, the mood within the paramilitaries and the UWC had changed dramatically.

By that time, many believed that victory had been handed to the stoppage organisers by what happened at return-to-work marches.

EIGHT

Early on the morning of Saturday 18 May Gerry Fitt received a phone call in his Belfast home from Merlyn Rees's office asking him to come across town for meetings. When the SDLP leader arrived, Brian Faulkner was already at Stormont and John Hume arrived soon afterwards by helicopter from his home in Derry. It was to be a day of crisis meetings aimed at setting up some kind of organisation at Stormont to deal with the stoppage.

Executive members were increasingly worried that the police and army seemed unable to deal with barricades and intimidation. They continued to hope that the stoppage would implode. So far little had emanated from the Northern Ireland Office and central government to help raise morale. Executive faith in the army was shattered, not just because of what was happening on the streets but because members had been told that, however qualified as engineers, soldiers were incapable of running the power system without the aid of civilian technicians. This was a bombshell. They knew that Vanguard leader, William Craig, had stated this the night before while leaving the meeting of Rees with loyalist politicians. Unless he was bluffing, it was safe to assume that the UWC and paramilitaries also knew the limitations of the army in the power stations.

The meetings at Stormont began. Hume complained that on one hand the Northern Ireland Office and its staff were meeting together while on the other, and separately, the Executive and its staff were meeting. If progress was to be made, then all meetings should be joint, he said.

Paradoxically this led to the widening of the split between the two centres because it led to two new committees being set up; one was to be ministerial to include Rees, Orme and Executive ministers with responsibility in areas relevant to matters at issue. Hume was a constant member because of electricity but Roy Bradford, the Environment Minister, would only be brought in if there were problems with water or sewage, for example.

The second emergency committee consisted of senior civil servants from each department and its function was to monitor the situation, gather information and furnish it to the politicians.

As it turned out, the civil servant committee played a more important role than that of the ministers because it had all the information rather than a digest. The ministerial meeting did not convene very often and never really got off the ground.

The central problem for all of them was how to give direction to the police and army but it soon became clear that the Secretary of State and officials of the Northern Ireland Office would not discuss security with members of the Executive.

John Hume understood this distrust because, along with others, he thought that at least one member of the Executive and some members of the civil servant committee had been leaking sensitive information to the UWC. The lack of any influence over security, particularly the police, was galling for Faulkner and his Unionist colleagues. Faulkner thought it extraordinary that the Executive should have the responsibility of maintaining electricity supplies yet be barred from discussions as to how to maintain the safety of power workers who might wish to work. It was a hopeless situation. When the Executive was unanimous in wanting the barricades ripped away, it was powerless to have this done. Afterwards Faulkner said that no moderate Unionist would ever participate again in a regional government in Belfast that does not have control over the police force. At least that was one point where he and the loyalists agreed.

So the achievement of that first Saturday, three and a half days after the announcement of the stoppage, was to set up some kind of organisation within government to deal with the crisis.

Hume could not get home that night because his driver was on strike, not that it made sense to return to Derry when Sunday promised to be busy. The slow-motion Ulster sabbath could not disguise the toll the strike had taken from normal life. Belfast's two power stations virtually stopped at lunchtime leaving Ballylumford at Larne to produce a mere third of the electricity needed. How long it could continue doing even that was a matter of conjecture. The power station had been without maintenance workers for much of week and was described officially as running at considerable risk. Electricity spokesmen were warning that the situation was now critical, a statement that appeared entirely believable to a province with so little electricity. In the north west, the rota was four hours electricity, twelve without. Elsewhere it was three on, seven off except in Belfast where it was ninety minutes on and five hours off.

Hospitals began sending less critical patients home. Heavy rain on Saturday brought fears of sewage emerging from the drains because the pumps were not operating fully. Queues lengthened at the petrol stations which could manually operate their pumps and garage owners tightened their unofficial rationing.

At noon Rees at long last declared a State of Emergency in response to a UWC threat to bring the remaining power workers out at midnight. He announced that the State of Emergency would empower him to send troops into the province's five power stations. He added that a small group of specially trained soldiers had been flown in and were standing by in case there was a complete blackout. The move was bluff. The Northern Ireland Office already had the power to put troops into the power stations if it wished, or to take any exceptional measures it thought necessary to maintain essential services. Furthermore, as Executive members had been told the day before, army personnel were not capable of running the grid.

Rees boarded a plane and flew to the Prime Minister's country residence at Chequers, ostensibly to obtain 'full endorsement and authority' for his actions. Perhaps so, but it was also likely that Cabinet colleagues would be asking questions as to whether the Executive was equal to the fight, especially if all electricity was withdrawn and government reduced to a matter of out-staring opponents.

The Executive had issued a statement of support for the emergency powers but, knowing that the measure would be interpreted as meaning that troops would enter the power stations, it tried between the lines to warn that government did not have an immediate answer to full electricity closedown.

As required by the situation, the Executive will of course act in any way open to them to protect life and minimise hardship; but it must be pointed out that in the event of the totally irresponsible and callous action of the kind which is now threatened, there is no means by which great hardship, even suffering to innocent members of the community can be averted.

The hidden portent of this message passed largely unheeded, for most people were taking it for granted that the army could work power stations. Those who gave the subject some serious thought worried more about the hundreds of miles of unprotected power lines and how long they would remain in place if the army entered the power stations.

The possibility of sabotage if soldiers did anything to maintain essential services was certainly occupying the minds of the GOC, Sir Frank King, and Sir Jamie Flanagan, the Chief Constable, when they conferred that Sunday afternoon with Orme.

That Sunday Gerry Fitt went to Cushendall on the Antrim coast for a meeting of the SDLP assembly party and some senior party officials. They discussed what they should do if the Executive fell. Party members clamouring for the army to restore full electricity supplies were silenced by the revelation from their leader that the army could not do it. Fitt privately had begun to wonder how committed the British government was to the Executive. He had heard that the Prime Minster, Harold Wilson, was to make a ministerial broadcast and was disappointed when it did not materialise.

The UUUC leadership was also meeting and the outcome was yet another blow against the Executive. The Vanguard, Democratic and Official Unionist parties, along with the Orange Order, had been resisting a publicly closer association with the UWC, and particularly with the paramilitaries. This caution was now thrown to the winds with a declaration of full support for the UWC. The UUUC steering committee said it was

appalled at the intransigence of the Secretary of State even to the extent of refusing to seek an agreement with no political conditions attached, which would have enabled essential services to be maintained with the help of the workers concerned.

The committee sees this as a rather drastic indication that it is the policy of the government to ride roughshod over the will of the majority of the people of Ulster in the implementation of the Sunningdale and the 1973 Constitution Act, regardless of cost.

The committee has noted with disgust that so-called Unionists under the leadership of Mr Faulkner are prepared to defy the will of the people thus making inevitable the present confrontation with government.

The committee in these circumstances has decided to give full support to the Ulster Workers' Council in an all-out effort to bring a change in Government policy. Members and organisations are asked to give immediate effect to this decision.

The loyalist politicians were now ready to gamble that the UWC would win. Why? Craig, Paisley and West knew by Sunday 19 May that the mood among ever more people was changing from uncertainty through acquiescence to support. The stoppage was depending less and less on intimidation.

The UWC had also been meeting that Sunday. Its meeting began in Hawthornden Road at the usual time of ten o'clock in the morning with Harry Murray in the chair because Glen Barr was not in Belfast. However, their attention was directed more towards agriculture than to the electricity question on the lips of everyone outside.

On Saturday the UWC had called for a complete stoppage from midnight on Sunday because the Secretary of State was refusing to negotiate. It was generally assumed that power stations were included in this blanket instruction but later both Murray and Pagels denied that any decision had been taken that weekend to bring all power to a halt. The absence of a decision reflected a split in the UWC between those who wanted the 'sudden death' of a complete blackout and those who wanted to graduate the pressure with a slow reduction. This argument continued as the supposed midnight Sunday deadline approached.

UDA commander Tyrie recalled the discussions.

What happened that particular night was this. Billy Kelly said power could be brought right down within a couple of hours and I replied, 'Why not say that power could be brought down within twelve hours, giving yourself some room to move?'

I had been listening to him [Kelly] earlier on saying that . . . you have to be very careful in case you destroy the machinery. . . . If you took the power too low, it could destroy the coils and put the machinery out of action for three months, or even a year.

Some said 'What about the hospitals?' I said that if you start worrying about those things at this stage, the strike is finished. Others said, 'What about the public? The public will kick up.' I said they won't. They'll blame it on the government because that's the way their minds are thinking. They'll say everything that's happening is the government's fault.

Tyrie's argument won the day, which perhaps was hardly surprising, given who he was. A statement was issued saying that power supplies would be continued at a level high enough to ensure the safety of the system. The UWC called once more for fresh elections and a complete shutdown of all business premises until this demand was granted.

Yet another blow struck the Executive that Sunday. Roy Bradford was with Faulkner, Fitt, Hume and Frank Cooper, the permanent under-secretary, having tea and sandwiches at Stormont Castle while waiting for civil service reports. An argument developed between Bradford and the others over the question of whether negotiation might be possible. Bradford was saying that some lines of communication with the strikers ought to be opened. To the rest Bradford was preaching heresy. Bradford felt so strongly he went immediately after the exchange to Cooper's office in an effort to sway the Northern Ireland Office but got nowhere. Tempers became so frayed that in the end Bradford said that if the rest persisted in their attitude they might find the Environment Minister himself on the Newtownards Road.

Bradford felt later that he should have resigned at that point. Instead he issued a public statement making plain his fundamental disagreement with the rest of the Executive and with the Northern Ireland Office.

> The Sunningdale agreement was never at any time unconditional. If the strikers and those who support them are saying that the Council of Ireland should not be implemented until the people have had a chance to give their verdict at the polls, there is solid sympathy for this view among pro-assembly Unionists, who in fact for many weeks have been thinking along the same lines. It follows therefore that the Secretary of State should be encouraged to re-open lines of communication with the Ulster Workers' Council, not to capitulate but to examine the viability of their viewpoint and to seek to remove deeply held fears which have absolutely no foundation in reality.

The rest of Bradford's colleagues were deeply dismayed at this disclosure about the possibility of amending the Council of Ireland provisions. Bradford had broken ranks publicly.

****

Monday 20 May. In the UWC headquarters the final organisation behind the stoppage took form. A smaller co-ordinating committee was set up consisting of the commanders of the various paramilitary organisations, three members of the UWC, three loyalist politicians, Jim Smyth of the UWC as the committee's press officer and Glen Barr as chairman. About fifteen members, though the number tended to vary. But at all times, the UWC was within it a small minority and the paramilitaries in the ascendancy. Thereby the basic nature of the strike became plain for all those with eyes to see.

Up until this point this smaller committee had existed as a steering body but its decisions needed ratification by the larger body—a time-consuming process. Henceforth the role of the larger committee was executive, becoming a means of transmitting orders down the many chains of command.

Monday's meeting began without the politicians present and the discussion centred on how the pressure on the authorities could be intensified. From his chairman's seat, Barr saw Paisley approaching. The DUP leader had difficulty in getting into the room because the guards had not yet been told that the UUUC leaders were now members of the co-ordinating committee. Notwithstanding the public support from the politicians, which was of very recent origin, some resentment remained because of their attitude during the beginning of the strike. One of the reasons the inner committee decided to publish its membership was to counter the impression that the politicians were the guiding hand. There was to be no easy leaping upon the bandwagon now that it was rolling with greater ease.

The three political leaders were held in varying degrees of regard by the UWC. William Craig's stock was highest because they thought his attitude had been more consistent. Harry West was next partly because he did not try to interfere too much except to champion the plight of farmers. Paisley came bottom and was trusted by committee members the least.

So that morning Paisley was kept deliberately outside the door. There was a suspicion about his journey to Canada to attend the funeral of a friend the previous week. There were those who thought the DUP leader had leapt at the chance to leave the province during the messy first days.

The lack of goodwill towards him manifested itself in the committee in various ways, such as the occasion when Paisley asked for a permission to run a bus from the city centre to the midweek service at his church on the Ravenhill Road. All bus services except those serving Catholic areas (over which the strike committee had no control) had been brought to a halt. Paisley's request was refused. Tyrie said he would reconsider if he was allowed to take the collection in the famous Free Presbyterian manner—silently (banknotes only) in plastic buckets.

Belfast Airport at Aldergrove, the province's only airport at the time, remained open throughout the strike, though closing it by withdrawing ground staff had been discussed. As a member of the Westminster parliament, Paisley needed air transport to London and back and he raised this point. One reaction was a stage whisper from Tommy Lyttle of the UDA, 'It's true then. He can't walk on water.'

On Monday Paisley was making his first appearance since returning from Canada. The meeting broke for coffee and when Barr returned to the room he found Paisley in the chairman's seat. Barr tapped Paisley on the shoulder and said, 'You might be chairman of the Democratic Unionist Party but I'm the chairman of the co-ordinating committee, so move over.'

Paisley did so, but took the chair with him. It was the only one with arms.

'You're still in my chair,' Barr said. The message was that Paisley was not to be allowed to take over the committee or the strike. Barr retained the chairmanship, though on this occasion, Paisley retained the chair.

Harry Murray was optimistic. On that Monday morning he believed that there would be a last-minute change of heart at Stormont Castle and that at any time there would be a phone call from a civil servant saying that another meeting with Rees was possible. He believed that government was being subjected to almost unbearable pressure.

This Monday was the day Tyrie thought the strike ought to have started. It would have been easier for him to have reached the position on the streets now extant. Only the most determined stood a chance of getting to work. Motorists who tried to argue their way past barricades sometimes found their cars becoming part of the barricade they were objecting to. Others managed to avoid barriers by entering the city through Catholic Andersonstown and the Falls Road which, like a wedge-shaped piece of pie, offered a zone of free passage to the centre. But for many such trouble was not worth it. Their places of work were all too often closed when they arrived.

The most serious worry for supporters of the government was that the army seemed happy to stand aside. People saw soldiers actually witnessing the hijacking of vehicles for barricades and doing absolutely nothing about it, or saw soldiers ignoring complaints from people trying to negotiate a blocked street. The impression was rapidly gained that the army was acquiescing in the collapse of normal order.

In mitigation, this state of affairs was not novel in Northern Ireland. The famous 'no-go' areas of the Bogside and Creggan in Derry existed so long that the barricades became concrete structures. At the time of the stoppage, much of the border area of south Armagh was one in which the army did not have full freedom of movement and from which the police had for all practical purposes withdrawn. Indeed in south Armagh government seemed to have tacitly recognised the limited extent of its control by pulling customs posts back from the border. As might be imagined, lack of full customs activity was not the subject of sustained public complaint but it was part of a process which rationalised the upholding of the law in peaceful parts and the flouting elsewhere. In a sense, the strike-bound areas were just bigger areas of lawlessness than had ever gone before.

By now it was a massive and passive revolt.

At half past two on Monday afternoon, 20 May, the Executive met in the Cabinet Room in Parliament Buildings at Stormont. If the Executive had survived, this meeting would have been regarded as putting one of its main foundations in place.

The meeting began with Merlyn Rees reading a statement to be delivered by Stanley Orme in the Commons at Westminster later that afternoon. Gerry Fitt had just emerged from a meeting with Rees and Faulkner and was in a very depressed mood. The lack of action against the stoppage loomed large in his thoughts. He realised that as a consequence of that inaction moderate Catholic as well as Protestant support for the Executive was withering and he passed a note to John Hume saying that the Executive might very well fall that evening.

Fitt was being over-pessimistic but it was understandable in the light of what Rees was saying at that moment. He was telling them in effect that bluff was to be continued, that extra troops were being drafted in but there was no intention of using them because to do so would erode the support the Executive already had. His words were received in stony silence. The remarks were interpreted as meaning that central government was refusing to back them. Small wonder Fitt thought the Executive was doomed.

When the agenda moved on the law enforcement report on extradition (the product of a joint UK/Ireland commission) which Rees would be discussing in cabinet in Downing Street on Thursday, it seemed irrelevant. In any case, Faulkner was not looking forward to the publication of that report since it advocated a policy unacceptable to his party.

Rees started talking about general support for the Sunningdale agreement when suddenly he began to talk about the Council of Ireland, which lay at the heart of loyalist opposition.

'I would ask you to treat as a matter of urgency what you are going to do about the Council of Ireland,' he told the Executive. He went on to say that it was urgent that the Executive announce an agreement that day. He said that if members came to an agreement it would only take effect if the Sunningdale agreement was signed. He was now telling the Executive to clear the way for the ratification of Sunningdale.

At last the attitude of the British government was becoming obvious to the Executive. Gently but firmly the Executive had been delivered an ultimatum. If London was to confront the loyalists, thereby risking a double-fronted guerrilla war against both Protestant and Catholic paramilitaries, the price must be the ratification of the Sunningdale agreement, modified if necessary. Anything less was not worth going to the wall for.

The words were of the greatest importance. Rees was rocking the Executive boat deliberately as a test of stability; if the boat sank, then it would have been proved unequal to the tasks facing it.

For weeks the Executive had been battling about the Sunningdale agreement and how it could be modified to a point where Faulkner's assembly party could accept it, the process Bradford had blown the whistle on. The SDLP was aware that Faulkner was walking a tightrope. If he fell, everything fell.

A sub-committee of the Executive had been formed to thrash out the problems of ratification. Its members were Roy Bradford and Leslie Morrell for the Faulkner Unionists, John Hume and Paddy Devlin for the SDLP and Bob Cooper of Alliance. During the preceding weeks the sub-committee had reached a position of deadlock, nearly always because the two hardliners, Bradford and Devlin, locked horns.

On the previous Friday the feeling between these two ministers reached the point of impasse. Bradford had made a remark interpreted by Devlin to mean that the sub-committee existed to accommodate the Unionist Party by staging the Sunningdale provisions over a period. Devlin lost his temper and told Bradford in forceful language that the purpose of the sub-committee was to discuss the problem and negotiate accordingly. He called Bradford many names and Bradford began packing his briefcase to leave. He was eventually persuaded to stay.

The other members of the sub-committee thought that this constant row would dictate failure eventually. Morrell, the Agriculture Minister, told both men on more than one occasion that he would knock their heads together. John Hume became so depressed as the battle raged about him that he buried his head in his hands on the table.

Bradford believed that the original negotiations at Sunningdale had been badly handled on the part of the Faulkner Unionists, resulting in an unworkable agreement. He believed that the SDLP had handled their negotiations most skilfully and had thereby achieved more than they were rightfully due. Some senior SDLP members privately agreed with that assessment and were ready to retreat a little in order to salvage most of what had been achieved. But Devlin was not one of these. He and others in the administration, including some Unionists, believed Bradford wanted to scrap most of the Sunningdale agreement.

Incredibly, and in spite of all this, by Monday 20 May an outline agreement to phase the implementation of Sunningdale was in place but no further progress could be made because other Executive members could not be sure of what Bradford would do.

The SDLP was ready to abandon the setting-up of a full Council of Ireland with executive powers and two parliamentary tiers until the next election for the Northern Ireland assembly in 1977–8. In the meantime they would accept a Council consisting of seven ministers from each part of Ireland. They would have co-ordinating functions over social, economic and police policies. In doing this the SDLP leadership was aware that it might be fashioning a block for its own head. Would SDLP party members agree that retreat should have been made to help out the Faulkner Unionists?

If the SDLP was to agree to a phasing along those lines it would need assistance from other parties in the Executive in the presentation of the deal. There would be no difficulty with the Alliance Party since their policy was to aid agreement. There would be no difficulty with most of the Unionist Party leadership.

Except Bradford.

It will be remembered that in the elections to the assembly, the Unionists had campaigned under an ambiguous manifesto which stated, 'Unionists are not prepared to participate in government with those whose primary object is to break the union with Great Britain.' The party split and the Faulkner section participated in government with the SDLP, a party whose undoubted long-term aim was the constitutional dissolving of the union of Great Britain and Northern Ireland.

Bradford considered he had been put in an impossible situation because of the ambiguity and stated afterwards that he would never allow himself to be put in a similar position ever again.

This goes some way towards explaining Bradford's attitude towards the projected agreement between the Unionists and the SDLP about Sunningdale. The SDLP had agreed to allow Sunningdale to be watered down, but if their action was represented as such it could provoke grass-roots opposition within the SDLP. So nobody, especially the Unionists, was to refer to a 'watering-down' of Sunningdale; the Unionists must not represent the phasing as a victory.

In this Bradford saw yet another ambiguous platform in the making and made it plain he would be placing his own interpretation on the phasing agreement. In other words, the nightmare confronting the SDLP was that Bradford would be able to argue that the Faulkner Unionists were refusing to ratify the Sunningdale agreement and amazingly the SDLP were willing to turn a blind eye. Bradford could make it read as if the SDLP were willing to put an Irish dimension on as long a finger as Irish unity itself in return for office in within the United Kingdom.

The SDLP leadership was very alarmed.

Rees was aware of this situation. That Monday he was telling the Executive to sort themselves out. There was a hint that the Cabinet in London thought the Sunningdale issue should have been sorted out before the February general election.

But everybody was stuck with the situation as it was. The SDLP used a statement from Seamus Mallon, party chairman, to call for Bradford's dismissal in strong terms, accusing him of indulging in a despicable form of political treachery. 'If he will not act in solidarity with his colleagues, then he should not be allowed to continue as a member of the Executive,' the statement said baldly.

The sentiments might have been expressed by Faulkner himself but he contented himself with making it publicly known that there was a basic disagreement between himself and his Environment Minister. He was in a precarious position. His own backbenchers met and declared that they agreed with Bradford. They issued a statement which confirmed to the population at large that talks about watering down Sunningdale had been taking place. Furthermore they said that if the SDLP had moved position earlier, the loyalist strike might never have happened. The cracks were widening.

****

On Monday 20 May the UWC requested all milk and bread delivery men to return to work as essential services. The Belfast Co-operative Society sent out twenty milk delivery lorries and none returned. A bacon factory took delivery of 750 pigs for slaughter but could not kill them because of the shortage of power. On the other hand it did not have enough food to keep them alive.

Farmers continued to poured thousands of gallons of milk into the drains, but now kept careful note of the quantities because they were to be paid for it all. Housewives were warned against using unpasteurised milk; if they bought any milk from open containers it should be boiled for three minutes.

Hospitals were beginning to worry about fuel for their emergency generators and once again reminded all non-urgent cases that they would not be admitted. They remained open for maternity and casualty treatment.

In Larne control passed almost totally to the paramilitary organisations who kept the port and most of the town sealed off. To hammer the lesson home, a hundred hooded men in paramilitary dress stood in ranks outside the police station for half an hour while a deputation of men responding to military-style orders met senior police officers to complain about the ill treatment of one of their members at the hands of the police.

One of the three generating sets still operating at Ballylumford power station developed a fault and an appeal was made for more workers to run up another set. Power was now at such a low level that a fault could trip the system out and cause sudden collapse. Hume warned, 'If this were to take place, Northern Ireland would be in the position of having no electricity supplied for a protracted period of time and would be faced with the gravest consequences.' The strike organisers already knew that.

The Post Office, which ran the telephone services, warned that telephones might be cut off with the exception of emergency calls. Meanwhile all postal services in Belfast had been halted and only emergency telegrams were being delivered.

Paddy Devlin topped the gloom by saying that the social services system was breaking down.

> Staff have been prevented from reaching their offices to deal with the many thousands of claims for unemployment benefit. Further, in the Belfast area the Post Office is unable to collect Giro cheques issued by the department for delivery to beneficiaries, and individual post offices are unable to draw money from the banks to cash Giro cheques and order books already in the hands of beneficiaries. If this situation continues, not only will people thrown out of work by the present strike be unable to collect benefit due to them and their families, but scores of thousands of old-age pensioners and sick people will also be unable to cash their paying instruments.

Merlyn Rees was working on a plan. He had decided to raise his colours over the 'back-to-work' marches the following morning, the ones organised by the trade union movement, the ones Britain's top trade unionist, Len Murray, was lending his presence and support to. Len Murray arrived in Northern Ireland this Monday and Rees saw him twice. As he did so, Garrett and McIldoon of the Northern Ireland Labour Party, along with others, were manning telephones convening a community conference of 'moderates'.

These people were clergymen, medical doctors and consultants, substantial businessmen like Peter Simms and Peter Brand, academics from Queen's University in Belfast like Alan Milne, Professor of Social Philosophy, Barry White, leader writer of the Belfast Telegraph, Denis Barritt, secretary of the Belfast Council of Social Welfare. From politics were David Bleakley, an ex-Minister of Community Relations in Northern Ireland (and the first and only Labour Party member to accept a post in a Unionist administration), Robin Baillie, Unionist ex-Minster of Commerce, Peter McLachlan, prominent Faulkner Unionist backbencher. Also, Sandy Scott, the well-known shop steward in the shipyard.

The fact that such people were trying to bring about talks of some description should have warned Stormont that the authorities were losing the hearts-and-minds battle. There might be some excuse for the English politicians, new to the game, and their Northern Ireland Office civil servants whose administration was colonial in character. But no such explanation is open to Executive members.

The mood was changing rapidly. These 'moderates' knew in their bones that the two-pronged trade union march on Tuesday morning was likely to be an embarrassing flop. As Garrett put it shortly after the strike, 'I think we all knew it was going to be a disaster and there was much discussion about this. People who were entirely in support of the union with Great Britain or steeped in Unionism knew it was going to be a farce. They knew there was no support for it.'

****

Throughout the night of Monday and into the fateful morning of Tuesday 21 May both sides issued their battle orders. The trade union marches were widely advertised as taking place from Queen's Quay to the shipyards and from Grand Parade to the Castlereagh industrial estate. Both were short routes and both were timed for a quarter to eight in the morning.

In a final rallying call the trade union movement said on Monday night that they demanded the right to work and expected all employers to respond by ensuring that places of work were open. 'We have told the Secretary of State that work people wish to return to work tomorrow. He has assured us that security forces will do all they can to make this possible.'

The UWC called the Irish Congress trade unionists communists and allies of the republican movement. 'The Secretary of State has agreed to subsidise the expenses of all these people if they are successful in breaking the constitutional stoppage, or if they can substantially denigrate it,' it accused and added confidently, 'We don't have to ask for your support. We have it and you have let us know we have it.'

The paramilitaries did not share Harry Murray's conviction that the marches could be left to fail through support for the cause. Tyrie knew the UWC people were perfectly capable of deluding themselves. He had not forgotten those opening days of the strike.

The Belfast morning daily newspaper, the *News Letter*, which had a largely Protestant readership published the tactics of the UDA. It reported that all main roads in the province were to be barricaded from six o'clock in the morning and no one was to be allowed through except medical services. Everyone was advised to remain in their home areas and make no attempt to go to work or school.

In an effort to keep the roads open, the authorities put 1,500 troops and several hundred police (the police only ever had 1,500 men stationed in Belfast out of a total force of 4,300 and were 2,000 under strength) into the city at midnight and claimed to have kept open nine main routes into the city. To have been fully effective, however, they would have needed to patrol several large Protestant housing estates and warrens of little streets with terraced housing. Since this was impossible with the resources at their command, keeping the main routes open was an empty achievement. People who wanted to work didn't reach those routes. Furthermore the paramilitaries were using mobile barriers, human chains or cars hastily parked across carriageways. These would be removed when soldiers or policemen appeared and reappear when they had gone. It would have needed a far larger force of troops to establish freedom of movement in east Belfast alone.

The main march was planned from Queen's Quay to the shipyard and was to be led by Len Murray of the TUC. Fifteen minutes before it was due to begin only a handful of people had arrived and few of them were workers. Many were sympathisers with the Executive, such as the Woman Together organisation and the Rev. Joseph Parker of the Witness for Peace movement. He was carrying his famous banner depicting a multitude of small crosses and the latest number of deaths caused by the most recent troubles. At that time it stood at 1,024, one of them being his own 14-year-old son.

The sad, sincere and small group numbered less than 200 and was a far cry from the dungareed throng some optimists hoped to see. The TUC general secretary, Len Murray, had at his side Andy Barr, president of the Federation of Shipbuilding and Engineering Workers and Jimmy Graham, Amalgamated Engineering Union general secretary. Flanked by soldiers and policemen they ran the gauntlet of a large jeering and booing crowd throwing eggs, stones and pieces of metal. One woman managed to land a blow on Len Murray himself. A group of loyalist youths blocked the entrance to the harbour estate gates and security forces fought, pushed and wrestled for five minutes before a way could be forced through for the marchers.

Once inside Len Murray praised the courage of the small band, telling them that he had now experienced for himself the type of intimidation which people living in Northern Ireland were subjected to. The man was visibly shaken.

The other back-to-work march at Castlereagh was even more of a debacle. Seventeen men and two women took part. Again a loyalist crowd, among them Glen Barr, made life difficult for the marchers, who included David Bleakley of the Labour Party and Robin Glendinning, the Alliance Party organiser.

It was noted bitterly that at both the marches there were barriers across the roads very near to the assembly points and the police and army made no effort to clear them. Glendinning thought the Secretary of State had let them all down. In front of reporters he shouted, 'It was time the Welsh wizard Merlyn Rees pulled his finger out and got the barricades down.'

Glen Barr was delighted at the miserable collapse of the marches and in his euphoria stated that in his personal opinion it would be possible for the stoppage organisers to set up their own provisional government. That statement caused great alarm at Stormont and Westminster.

Why was the failure so complete? Attempts to put it all down to intimidation began to be embarrassing; there was a limit to how many would accept that there had been a point-one per cent turn-out because ninety-nine-point-nine per cent had been intimidated. Why had the Northern Ireland Office mistakenly been setting so much store by the Irish Congress of Trade Unions? The reason was articulated in a bulletin published by the Workers' Association, which supported the stoppage.

In Britain there is at least a general identity of broad political sympathy between the TUC and the mass of trade unionists.

This is not so in Northern Ireland. Andrew Barr, chairman of the Shipbuilding Confederation and Jimmy Graham of the AEU led the back-to-work campaign. They are anti-partitionists. The bulk of their members are Unionists. [Andrew] Barr and Graham are heeded by the rank and file in trade union affairs proper, but when they led the back-to-work campaign, they were not acting as trade union members but as politicians. In political matters they are at loggerheads with their members, so the campaign failed. . . .

There is a tacit understanding in the trade union movement that political and economic matters will be kept separate. In circumstances of sharp political division this is a necessary condition for keeping the trade union movement united in economic matters. Barr, Graham, etc. broke this convention . . . and it is this fact, rather than intimidation on the housing estates that caused this morning's fiasco.

Sandy Scott, who had received public honour for his efforts to keep sectarianism at bay in the shipyard, and who did not support the UWC, agreed with that view. So did Brian Garrett, who as chairman of the Northern Ireland Labour Party had good knowledge of the labour movement. He said at the time, 'Any bloody fool could have told them [Stormont] that there were not going to be many men turning up, basically because the trade unions that were leading it had never held shop floor meetings on constitutional issues. They had the sympathy of decent men, but as armchair trade unionists they were out of touch and even a menace to positive action.'

Scott said that Len Murray had been furious because he thought he had been misled by the Irish Congress of Trade Unions Northern Committee. A few days after the strike had ended, Garrett met Lord Feather, who as Vic Feather had been Len Murray's predecessor at the TUC. Lord Feather had told him that a number of trade union leaders in Great Britain, having watched what happened, realised that he had been 'sold a pup' by the Northern Committee and now saw that the government was attempting to solve a constitutional dispute as if it were an industrial one.

The trade union movement in the province was damaged and the episode marked the final nail in the coffin of the Northern Ireland Labour Party. However, those were side effects. More important was the tremendous blow to the credibility of the Executive and the Secretary of State. As the first substantial move against the stoppage it was a colossal miscalculation. A large proportion of the Protestant middle classes now believed more than ever that the authorities were inept, confused, misinformed, tentative and ultimately, powerless. Government was going to lose.

'That's good. The war's over,' an ecstatic Harry Murray shouted. He was wrong. It was not over yet.

NINE

The failure of the marches had one immediate effect unknown to most at the time. It wrecked the attempts to persuade the UWC that negotiations could be a way of achieving any of their aims.

The strike co-ordinating committee was triumphant and all doubts and indecision evaporated. Joe Barkley was a stager shop steward in the shipyard and a member of the UWC Belfast committee. Sandy Scott knew him and was trying to open lines of communication with the UWC through him.

On the Tuesday morning of the failed marches, Scott was at Barkley's house in the Shankill area of Belfast to tell him that a group was working behind the scenes to find a way of ending the stoppage and that they had contacts with the Northern Ireland Office. Scott was urging Barkley to make it easier for Rees to entertain talks. He had reached the point of making arrangements for a deputation to go to the UWC to argue this point when the radio was turned on. Both men listened to the BBC account of what was happening at the shipyard. As it unfolded Scott realised that the time for his suggestion was passing like dry sand through his hands. Barkley was cock-a-hoop.

In another part of the city Gerry Fitt was listening to the same broadcast in his home. The previous night he had told some colleagues on the Executive that he expected army action during the night to clear the barricades. Rees and Orme would tell trusted members of the Executive some security-sensitive information informally and outside Executive meetings. Neither the Northern Ireland Office nor the army trusted everyone in the Executive or the Northern Ireland civil service.

On the seven o'clock news that morning, Fitt expected to hear that all roads were open. Instead there seemed to be more barricades than ever. On the eight o'clock news he heard that eggs had been thrown at Len Murray and the marches had become victories for his enemies.

A telephone call asked him to go to Stormont immediately in a helicopter waiting at Girdwood military camp beside his home on the Antrim Road. As he walked through the soldiers to the aircraft he believed that he and the Executive had been left without support because the army had been unwilling to act. Faulkner was thinking along similar lines.

But neither of them full realised the sophistication of the paramilitary action on the streets. As Tyrie put it:

We had broken the thing's back. If we had over-reacted, messed people about and burned their motorcars, we were beaten. And yet if we didn't go on the streets to discourage people, we were still beaten. The most important thing people were saying to me was, 'We'll stick by you as long as there's no violence.' This was the strange thing—*as long as there was no violence.*

Some cars and lorries were nevertheless burnt and drivers were roughly handled while their cars were being taken from them, but on many occasions the vehicles were retrieved by police or army undamaged. Tyrie sincerely believed that the 'discouragement' campaign had been carried out with minimum force.

The following is an example of what was happening that Tuesday morning on the streets, as related by Tyrie. It demonstrated the nature of what the army and police were facing. One of the most serious threats of full-scale rioting occurred at Ballybeen, a Protestant housing area on the outskirts of Belfast where the UDA and the army were squaring up against each other ready for battle any minute. The UDA was determined to block the road; the army was determined to force it open. The confrontation was serious enough for Tyrie to be summoned from a strike co-ordinating committee meeting. When he reached Ballybeen he saw about 400 people facing nine armoured cars and three Land Rovers.

We had a meeting of all the UDA officers, funnily enough, in the back of a laundry van. But they had broken the rules. They had lined up, the usual thing, ready to go.

I told the [UDA] officers that they were doing exactly what the army wanted them to do. In a confrontation, an awful lot of people were going to get hurt and there would be bad publicity.

Break your men up into platoons, send them to different parts of the housing estate and have them on standby. Reduce your numbers. Let the army see you are organised.

But they couldn't understand this for a while, so I said, look it's as simple as this. If you are going to have a riot, let only a small platoon riot and it'll appear that the army is using its might against a small platoon of men.

Once he had his men on his side, Tyrie then went one step further.

I said, 'Who are you arguing with?' and they said, 'The army.' I said, 'Send for the police. The army will get so angry at being bypassed that they'll start arguing with the police, who will be asking for a compromise.'

So they sent for the police, talked to them and everyone came away quite happy. What they did was let the women stop cars with women in them and the men stop cars with men in them, and nobody interfered. This settlement took me half an hour.

There has never been any official confirmation that such an agreement was ever made but the account gives a picture of how Tyrie was conducting the battle. The strategy did have an effect. Violence was reduced to a point where normally law-abiding Protestants were not provoked. When it occurred, the organised UDA retreat from challenged barricades and the overall lack of rioting convinced the army that sufficient discipline was being enforced to evidence a coherent strategy. Army officers told politicians that this development worried them.

Back at Hawthornden Road Andy Tyrie was put in charge of all the sanctions the co-ordinating committee could apply, despite the opposition of the Rev. Ian Paisley, who thought Tyrie was too hardline. The politicians seemed to have been a moderating influence inside the committee, constantly advising against pushing people too far.

The collapse of the back-to-work marches meant that Tyrie and other hardliners could take advantage of a new confidence in the committee and push for more severe sanctions to bring the conflict to a head. So that Tuesday they decided to operate a complete embargo on oil and petrol supplies. This was announced at lunchtime.

Tyrie made an interesting observation about the way he operated in the committee. 'My problem was if you pushed your ideas too hard, people didn't want them. Or if you said too much in that room, others altered your thinking right away. You have to allow a certain amount of movement, allowing people to add to your ideas so that it becomes everybody's idea.' Tyrie was a formally uneducated man, a ruthless man and an intelligent effective man.

Harry West of the UUUC was a farmer in Fermanagh and knew well the problems facing farmers as the strike progressed. The milk producers had ceased to be a problem because they were to be paid whether they delivered or not, but they still had to feed their animals. The egg, chicken and pig producers were facing greater problems because Bob Pagels, the 'minister of agriculture' as he was known in the committee, was restricting the supply of feedstuffs. He dictated what went where from an office which the mill owners made available.

At the Tuesday meeting of the co-ordinating committee West was putting the case for the farmers very well, saying that they were willing to support the stoppage even though they had lost a certain amount. He was backed up by that day's newspapers with photographs of a farmer beside a hummock of 40,000 day-old chicks which the stoppage had caused to be slaughtered. This was bad publicity and lent weight to West's plea that animals should not suffer. The lunchtime statement also said the supply of pig and poultry animal food will resume at minimum levels.

But as Tyrie put it afterwards: 'My idea was to make people angry, but not too angry . . . so what you had to do was give them a concession, then take it off them. So you said, "Deliver your animal food," then you take the petrol away so they could not deliver. And you could say it was not your fault.'

Ruthless.

* *

Politicians on both sides of the Irish Sea met on Tuesday afternoon, 21 May, in their respective legislatures and the events in Ulster dominated.

The politicians supporting the Executive at Stormont were dejected, their mood made blacker because of a barricade across the road outside Parliament Buildings. Paddy Devlin, Minister for Social Services, announced the temporary removal of complicated checks which were made before sickness and unemployment benefit was paid. Henceforth, the existing flat rate, plus additions for dependants, would be given to all applicants, but not supplementary or earnings-related payments.

There was an argument at the time that by using all means within his power to pay unemployment benefit, Devlin was playing into the hands of his political enemies but Devlin's course of action was inevitable, given his background.

Paddy Devlin had been a very active member of the trade union movement. He had worked alongside several prominent UWC members in happier days when they were all members of the Northern Ireland Labour Party. Class loyalty did not permit a man like Paddy Devlin to stop unemployment benefit payments, whatever the circumstances. Nevertheless the payments would remove any remaining sanction against striking and, on the face of it, seemed a remarkable measure.

But the argument Devlin himself used was that nobody could be sure about the reason for every individual absence from the workplace. In the early days, massive intimidation was an undoubted cause.

In the initial period, we are talking about two or three per cent of the people who left work voluntarily and who imposed the stoppage on the rest. So I couldn't say give the benefit to that man and not this one because I could not work out who was responsible. The fairest way was to give to all who applied.

Early on we discovered in the ministry that only twenty-five per cent of our personnel were coming into work, so without the extra claims generated by the strike, we had problems meeting our normal 360,000 payments related to old-age pensions, the chronically sick and all other benefits.

Some staff who could not reach their offices went to the nearest local office and worked there, but this couldn't solve the problem. We thought at the time that we could get assistance from the employers, that they would open their offices, but they refused.

Then more complications. Normally we receive a claim at the counters of our various offices and send the information back by post to the government offices at Stormont for checking and matching. But this information wasn't getting back because the postal system had stopped and we don't use the telephone for that type of information. And even if we had managed somehow to overcome this problem, we still needed the Post Office to deliver the money drafts or Giro cheques.

Then we made an arrangement with the Post Office for special deliveries and were able to get this going after the third or fourth day of the stoppage. Then when we managed by those means to give people the drafts and Giros, the recipients found difficulty in cashing them. The banks were closed and there was no cash in the post offices. Clearly there was an enormous hold-up at four or five different points in the normal procedure. Short cuts had to be taken.

I made it clear that all claims were to be processed, quickly and generously, and I didn't care if there was an error in giving too much. I wanted to make certain it wasn't too little because the complaints were flowing in from old-age pensioners, one-parent families and social workers.

Afterwards when the case was made that many people did indeed receive too much in benefit, Devlin was unrepentant. He made his decision for the reasons stated and in the full knowledge that his department was a designated target of the strikers.

As Andy Tyrie said, 'The first week off work you get no social security since you would have your last week's wages. But during that first week we wanted everybody to queue outside the dole, thousands of them. . . . We wanted to block the whole system'.

So that afternoon, Devlin unblocked the system in so far as it lay in his power to do so. But his statement to the assembly at Stormont that afternoon demonstrated how much power had slipped from the Executive's grasp. Devlin was forced to appeal to the stoppage organisers to allow some of the functions of the government to continue.

'I would appeal to the men responsible for this situation, if they have any shred of humanity, to stop their sabotage of my department's operations. My staff must be allowed to do their job and the Post Office and banks must be permitted to Giro cheques and the money required to meet them and maintain payment against their order books.'

The system could only operate even to this foreshortened degree with the permission of the men in Hawthornden Road. The co-ordinating committee met and it allowed the payments. Who was governing, it became pertinent to ask?

Only the parties supporting the Executive were now attending the assembly and the strain was beginning to show. The SDLP chairman attacked David Bleakley for suggesting that somehow the loyalists must be brought into the Executive. While this went on, the lights went out for a short period. When they came on again, Mallon turned on Roy Bradford for suggesting negotiations. 'I must remind this man', he thundered, 'and his colleagues that political treachery is not forgotten no less than any other form of treachery.'

The fur was beginning to fly among those who should have been putting on a show of solidarity. The neatest debating point was scored by Peter McLachlan who quietly reminded many of the SDLP politicians of their own political beginnings. The SDLP front bench consisted largely of men who had risen to prominence through street politics and through demonstrations which often had broken the letter of the law. He asked them to recognise parallels.

There followed reports from various ministers. Hume confined his report to electricity, revealing that the Northern Ireland grid had been divided into two parts. Coolkeeragh power station now served only the north west, Ballylumford the south east. Both stations were operating with difficulty. He warned that the UWC embargo on oil might affect the production of domestic gas.

Faulkner gave a comprehensive review which a speech writer might describe as having no cheer-lines. Some roads were blocked, the meagre electricity supply was in danger because of a lack of maintenance, no petrol was reaching service stations, oil supply for hospital standby generators was at critical levels, industry was almost completely shut down, farmers were badly hit in many different ways, milk supplies were interrupted, all meat, bacon and poultry processing plants were shut, boats remained unloaded at the docks, school attendance was reduced, some water supplies were at risk, bus services and road haulage were in difficulty, street cleaning and refuse collection in Belfast had ceased, postal services had stopped in some areas, many sub-post offices had run out of money and there was the prospect of a sugar shortage.

Appropriately the lights went out during the speech.

At Westminster the leaders of the two main parties clashed over Northern Ireland for the first time in five years. The Conservative leader, Edward Heath, said he hoped the security forces would be used to clear the barricades. He recognised that the strike was political in nature.

He was unable to resist the temptation to make the same point that Harry Murray had used to taunt Stanley Orme. He contrasted the manner in which Labour in office was dealing with a political strike and how in opposition it had reacted to a political miners' strike in Britain some months ago. The miners' strike had the political aim of bringing down a statutory wage policy by Heath's Conservative government and the Labour Party had supported the miners. Heath said the Conservatives were prepared to support the Labour government since the Conservative Party was against political strikes.

The Labour leader and Prime Minister, Harold Wilson, replied that Mr Heath did not understand what was going on in Northern Ireland itself. 'This is not only a political strike, it is a sectarian strike aimed at destroying decisions taken by this House related to power sharing and by the elected assembly. It is being done for sectarian purposes which have no relation to this century—only to the seventeenth century.'

* *

On the night of Tuesday 21 May, one week after the declaration of the strike, two important meetings were held. Both in their own way demonstrated that the strike had taken root so securely that even bedrock supporters of the Executive began to smell defeat.

The largest meeting was that of the 'moderates', business and professional people mostly but not exclusively Protestant. It met in the Quaker Meeting House on the Lisburn Road in Belfast. This was the meeting that the NILP leaders, the New Ulster Movement and some churchmen had combined to arrange, making sure to emphasise that no party political emblem would be flying from the pole.

The organisers wanted to convince the government that it had lost the support of the moderates. The fiasco of the marches combined with government reaction which amounted to little more than tantrums and inaction had been the last straw, so when a hundred people of influence turned up they were in a mood to do more than talk. The chair was taken by Denis Barritt, secretary of the Belfast Council of Social Welfare and a lifelong dedicated reformer. He was a respected figure. He opened the meeting by saying that they needed to find a unanimous course of action and the discussion would therefore be confined to what could be done to stop power supplies from deteriorating. This would avoid divisions about constitutional issues.

Speaker after speaker demanded to know what the government was doing. The general feeling was that the government had not exhausted the possibilities of talking and that they could assemble a committee of sufficient weight to see Rees, Orme— even the Prime Minister.

A deputation was agreed: Denis Barritt himself, Robert Hurndell (Boilermakers Union), Professor Alan Milne, Dr Oliver Hunter (Catholic family doctor in east Belfast), Bishop Quinn (Church of Ireland Bishop of Down and Dromore), the Rev. John Stewart (Methodist Church and Northern Ireland Labour), Sandy Scott (convenor of shipyard trade unions), Peter Simms (Chairman, Gamble Simms Ltd), Mrs Nonie McClure (Women Together), the Rev. Derek McKelvie (Northern Ireland Council of Social Service) and Brian McGuigan (New Ulster Movement).

It is worth noting that Nonie McClure was Roman Catholic and known as a member of the Civil Rights Movement which had articulated Catholic and nationalist opposition to Unionist government in Northern Ireland. She made a passionate speech to the effect that just as Catholics once had a grievance, now the Protestants had one. This group left immediately as a delegation for Stormont where they handed in a short statement. It read:

> In this situation of imminent breakdown, we call upon all parties to the present dispute, including the Northern Ireland Executive (a) to meet at once for the purpose of safeguarding adequate electrical supply and (b) to explore all possible means not yet attempted of resolving the present deadlock. We are deeply concerned that the government should not depart from the traditional British practice of being willing to talk to all parties in any dispute. We further plead with the Ulster Workers' Council and the community at large to consider the dangers imminent in the present situations.

The duty officer at Stormont Castle dutifully took their piece of paper and the deputation left for Hawthornden Road, where they informed the UWC what they were doing. Harry Murray repeated that they were wasting their time because the government would not change its mind about talks, no matter how limited the agenda. He now knew that the Labour Party document had been rejected.

Murray apologised to the delegation for meeting them in darkness. The electricity was off, he explained.

Plans were now hurriedly laid for the deputation to travel to London the next day or Thursday. The deputation had gone as far as it could in Northern Ireland. Its members now felt they must convey as a matter of urgency what they regarded as the real truth of the situation to politicians in London.

The other meeting that night was openly party political. Eleven of the SDLP parliamentary party met in Belfast to decide whether or not to agree to the phasing of part of the Sunningdale agreement. The SDLP negotiators of the Executive sub-committee had conceded that a full Council of Ireland was not possible in the short term and that in the interests of preserving power sharing—and office—they should settle for less.

Hume and Devlin, the negotiators, were by now somewhat less fearful about what Bradford might do in terms of presentation of the phasing because Bradford had now openly broken with the Executive on the question of negotiating with the UWC. Bradford's aggressive interpretation of the phasing could now be attributed to his being out of step with the whole Executive.

If Bradford faded away as a problem for the SDLP, into his place stepped their own Paddy Devlin. He astounded the meeting by declaring that he himself, one of the people who had negotiated the compromise, was now against it. Not against the phasing itself, he explained, but against the timing of the announcement. In his view, releasing the news now would be regarded as retreat in the face of loyalist pressure and de facto negotiation with the UWC.

However, Devlin was not successful in carrying his argument that evening. Those present agreed with their leader, Gerry Fitt, that to attempt to achieve the Council of Ireland in its original form at the moment would lead to the downfall of Faulkner and that phasing was necessary. But the eleven men constituted just over half the parliamentary party and they decided have a full meeting of the assembly party the next day at noon.

The next day was to be the most revealing of the Executive's short history.

TEN

At three o'clock on Wednesday morning, 22 May, between 3,000 and 4,000 troops were deployed in an effort to open areas impassable for army patrols for two days.

Their instructions were to clear the roads, using tact rather than force. It was a move many said had come far too late. Unmanned barriers consisting of abandoned and hijacked vehicles were pushed aside. Manned barricades were talked out of existence, sometimes over a period of four hours. But once more, the Protestant paramilitaries made barricade removal a little like clay pigeon shooting. As one fell from sight, up popped another. It mattered little that by breakfast time many of the fixed barricades had gone. The were replaced by human chains of men, or even worse, women. The army discovered that cars and lorries were not the real substance of the barricades. So in spite of the army effort, Gerry Fitt had once more to be ferried from one part of Belfast to another to reach Stormont.

The SDLP meeting had been brought forward to half past eleven and an Executive meeting was fixed for the unusual hour of twelve midday. They usually began earlier.

Before either of these meetings, Faulkner took Fitt with him to meet Rees and they both told him the Executive could not carry on without meaningful support from the Northern Ireland Office. They told him that they expected to reach agreement on the phasing of the Sunningdale agreement that day, but that their effort would count for nothing unless the authority of government was re-established. Rees listened, but wanted the Sunningdale phasing in the bag before promising anything.

As it turned out, the prediction from the two leaders that agreement would be reached that day was wrong. When Gerry Fitt explained the proposal to a full meeting of SDLP assembly members, their reaction was hostile. The backbenchers had been envisaging a measure of phasing, perhaps a delay in setting up the Council until the end of the year, but not delay until after the next assembly election in 1977. The SDLP leaders realise too late that they ought to have prepared the ground with the backbenchers.

To no avail did Fitt tell them that the situation was really dangerous, that Faulkner was not bluffing. He warned that if the Executive collapsed during the UWC strike because of the SDLP attitude, they would be criticised unmercifully. As Hume put it, 'I know we will be in trouble with the constituencies for agreeing to a phasing, but if we decide otherwise, everything will be gone. We can't carry the Council of Ireland at the present time and that is the reality.'

After an hour and a half, the SDLP voted down the phasing agreement eleven votes to eight. Fitt told them very forcibly that their decision meant the end of power sharing in Northern Ireland. He left and headed for the room where the Executive was meeting. It was one o'clock.

Oliver Napier, the Alliance Party leader, recalled the moment.

None of the SDLP members had turned up for the Executive meeting and the grapevine had it that they were at a party meeting. The Executive had already reached agreement on phasing. I remember Gerry coming in. His face is always very readable and he was in very bad form, indeed almost on the verge of tears. The rest of the SDLP members came in.

Gerry said, 'It's no go. It's not on.' Turning to Faulkner he held out his two hands and said, 'I'm sorry, Brian, it's not on.'

The news hit Faulkner a hammer blow.

Faulkner called the meeting to order and Fitt formally announced that he could not carry his party with him on the matter of phasing. But Fitt was an incorrigible optimist and, before Faulkner could proceed with a vote that would have ended the Executive, Fitt asked for an adjournment to allow him to go back to the party once more.

So Fitt went back to the party meeting and asked for ten minutes of their time. Hitherto he had said that he believed that Faulkner was depending on an agreement on phasing and had no further room for manoeuvre. Now he told them that as a matter of fact, Faulkner was about to pull out of the Executive because of the SDLP vote. In the light of that knowledge, he asked for another vote on the issue.

The power-sharing Executive, together with officials and government ministers. *Left to right*: Frank Cooper (official), Leslie Morrell, Kenneth Bloomfield (official), Gerry Fitt, Robert Cooper, Eddie McGrady, William van Straubenzee (Minister of State), Austin Currie, Francis Pym (Secretary of State), Basil McIvor, Paddy Devlin, Herbert Quirke, John Baxter, Brian Faulkner, John Hume, Major Robert Lloyd Thompson, Oliver Napier, Ivan Cooper and Roy Bradford.

Above: A Co-op bread van. As the stoppage bit harder, food distribution became a problem, particularly in Belfast. This bread van became a mobile shop.

Below: The fate of this petrol station in Ballymena is a good illustration of how government became impotent. The station had been commandeered by the army as part of the oil plan, but stoppage supporters blockaded it.

Above: Without grain deliveries, farmers in the Protestant heartland had little option but to kill stock, in this case chickens a few days old.

Below: A coffin labelled Liam Cosgrave (mis-spelt), Gerry Fitt and Brian Faulkner. At the beginning of his political career, Faulkner could not possibly have foreseen such a demonstration against him by Unionists.

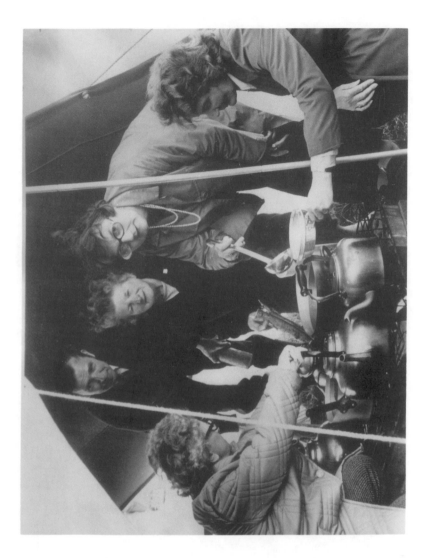

Communal cooking under canvas. A kind of 'London blitz' atmosphere pervaded, though whether it would have persisted beyond the two weeks of the UWC stoppage is an imponderable of history.

Back-to-work march. The back-to-work marches were dismal and public failures. For all the seeming effort at protection, relatively few workers appeared and those that did faced bitter intimidation from a host of hostile bystanders.

It was difficult to use even minimum force against a barricade which consisted of a line of women linking arms. RUC officers, as here in east Belfast, were embarrassed and often powerless to deal with them. And yet such barricades were as effective as any other.

A woman reading by oil light. By reducing electricity to the point where factories could not run, the UWC created a lock-out rather than a strike. At the end, even the oil for that lamp would have been in short supply.

Glen Barr, stoppage leader.

Faulkner and Rees.

These contemporary newspaper advertisements recall the realities of daily life during the stoppage in a particularly graphic way.

BELFAST CITY COUNCIL

GAS DEPARTMENT

We are sorry we cannot supply sufficient Gas to maintain normal pressure in the BELFAST, BANGOR, CARRICKFERGUS HOLYWOOD, LISBURN, NEWTOWNABBEY and NEWTOWNARDS Districts

PLEASE:

(1) TURN OFF YOUR GAS AT THE MAIN CONTROL TAP
which you will find beside the gas meter.

(2) TURN OFF ALL OTHER GAS TAPS
For example: Gas cooker taps and taps on pipes leading to gas appliances.

(3) DO NOT TURN ON THE GAS AGAIN
UNTIL YOU ARE TOLD TO DO SO by a similar announcement.

(4) IF IN DOUBT, LEAVE IT OUT

(5) HELP YOUR NEIGHBOUR
They may not know of this warning. Please tell them. Make sure the aged and the handicapped and those living alone are safe and know what to do.

To keep the gas system safe, some gas has to remain in the pipes. If you turn on your taps you may let air into your pipes —or someone else's. Air and gas together form an explosive mixture and turning on the taps too soon may result in an explosion in your home, or your neighbours, or in the street.

An open tap could let explosive amounts of gas into your home if the supply is restored without your knowledge, so **PLEASE DO AS WE ASK.**

27th May, 1974.   **J. M. BROWN, General Manager.**

EMERGENCY POWERS

Emergency Arrangements for Distribution of

OIL PRODUCTS

The Northern Ireland Executive has introduced compulsory arrangements to ensure the availability of oil product to essential consumers.

BULK CONSUMERS

The following is a summary of the activities which have been designated as essential to the life of the community.

GAS
ELECTRICITY
WATER AND SEWERAGE UNDERTAKINGS
HOSPITALS
MEDICAL AND PHARMACEUTICAL SUPPLIES
FOOD MANUFACTURE AND DISTRIBUTION
DAILY NEWSPAPERS
AGRICULTURE
PUBLIC TRANSPORT
POST AND TELE-COMMUNICATION SERVICES
BROADCASTING
CERTAIN GOVERNMENT AND LOCAL
AUTHORITY ACTIVITIES

Persons responsible for the carrying on of these activities and any other activity considered to be essential should, if they are unable to obtain supplies from normal sources, contact one of the following numbers.

BELFAST 54151

or

LONDONDERRY 65052

PRIVATE CARS AND VEHICLES

The petrol filling stations listed here have been requisitioned by the Department of Commerce and are designated as Government-authorised filling stations.

These filling stations will be opened between the hours of 11 a.m. and 3 p.m. on Monday to Friday to meet the needs of a very limited number of known persons, whose performance of services essential to the community requires, the use of private transport. These persons have already received or will shortly receive an issue of coupons for use at Government-authorised filling stations.

Other drivers who consider the use of a vehicle to be essential to the community or for urgent personal reasons may make personal application at a permit centre. A list of these will be published later. The vehicle registration book should be produced. Petrol can then be purchased at a Government-authorised filling station on production of the permit issued.

It is stressed that the Government is not introducing a general scheme of petrol rationing and that the Government-authorised filling stations will be available only to motorists in possession of coupons or permits. Motorists are not precluded from obtaining supplies of petrol from such normal sources as may be available.

GOVERNMENT-AUTHORISED FILLING STATIONS

BELFAST
Daly's Garage, 240 Falls Road
Castleton Filling Station, 471 Antrim Road
Shore Road Filling Station, 728 Shore Road
Balmoral Filling Station, 2 Upper Lisburn Road
Ladas Drive Service Station, Ladas Drive
Castleview Service Station,
629 Upper Newtownards Road
Ulster Garages, 48 Corporation Street
LARNE
Kilwaughter Filling Station, Kilwaughter
BALLYMENA
Seven Towers Filling Station, George Street
PORTADOWN
Tweenways Service Station, Corcrain
LISBURN
Saintfield Road Service Station
BANGOR
Bangor Filling Station (Pringle), Belfast Road
LONDONDERRY
Clooney Filling Station, Limavady Road
Strand Road Service Station, 90 Strand Road
OMAGH
J. Charleston & Sons (Omagh) Ltd., Derry Road
ENNISKILLEN
J.P. Topping & Co. Ltd., 12 Dublin Road
NEWRY
Rockfoot Service Station, Belfast Road
ARMAGH
Newry Road Filling Station
DUNGANNON
Maxol Filling Station, Ballygawley Road
COLERAINE
Millburn Garage, Millburn Road
DOWNPATRICK
Downpatrick Service Station, New Bridge Street

Brian Faulkner.

Left:Andy Tyrie on his way into Stormont Castle, 1974.

Below: Harry Murray, on the left, in a thoughtful mood at a victory rally at Stormont after the stoppage. Alongside him are other members of the Co-ordinating Committee, Bob Pagels, Bill Hannigan, Lt Col Edward Brush, Hugh Petrie and Ken Gibson.

Queuing for unemployment benefit in Belfast. The UWC planned to clog the unemployment benefit system and, paradoxically, was helped by the Executive which, by classifying the stoppage as an illegal lock-out rather than a strike, made the denial of benefit payment untenable.

A road blockade in east Belfast. This was typical of the kind of barricade with which the police and army had to deal.

Above: It was street party time in Protestant areas of Belfast. It occurred to the stoppage organisers that they might continue the strike in pursuit of further political aims, but people voted with their feet. The collapse of the Executive was the victory they sought.

Below: For the Executive, part of the unthinkable. Farmers, whose livelihoods were threatened by the stoppage, joined the rebellion and demonstrated the fact at Parliament Buildings, Stormont.

Right:
Glen Barr (left)
and Ian Paisley
celebrating
victory.

Left: Stan Orme,
Minister of State
during the strike.

So they voted again—and the figures were the same. Eleven to eight against phasing. Fitt was on the verge of tears.

Meanwhile the Executive meeting had adjourned and its members went their separate ways, some to the bar. Before they had time to take their drinks came the message that the Executive was to re-convene. Fitt and the other SDLP members entered the room and it was clear from their bearing that they had had no success. Fitt quietly confirmed this. A very emotional scene followed.

There were tears in Faulkner's eyes, and this in a man known for his public composure. He said, 'Emotion rarely comes into my life . . .'

Faulkner listened as tributes were paid to him. Men who throughout most of their political careers had opposed him tooth and nail, were now shaking him warmly by the hand. Austin Currie, who had verbally flayed him on so many public platforms during recent stormy years approached and said, 'Irrespective of what has happened in the past, I and my colleagues have respected you tremendously in the past five months.' Faulkner replied that he felt the same way about the SDLP members he had been working with. John Hume said, 'We have made a terrible mistake but that is the way it is.'

Roy Bradford stood aloof. He thought the tears were out of place.

* *

As he was leaving the room, Fitt lifted the little placename tag with his name on it, wrote the time and date on it, slipped it into his pocket and walked out into the corridor. The others had disappeared. He looked at the policeman on security duty and told him it was all over.

What happened next belongs to the realm of the political thriller. Fitt suddenly had a brain wave. He signalled his bodyguard (they all had bodyguards) to accompany him, sped past two foreign journalists, telling them that things were looking very dark, and headed towards Stanley Orme's office in Stormont Castle, some 400 metres from Parliamentary Buildings. Fitt's connection with Orme stretched back to 1967 when he had brought him over to Northern Ireland. Now Fitt was able, on the basis of that long association, to ask Orme to talk to the SDLP. Orme agreed and the two men returned to Parliament Buildings in Fitt's car.

Word quickly passed through the dining room and bar that the SDLP meeting was being re-convened and all the assembly members turned up to hear Orme. Partly because he could not bear the suspense and partly because he thought it the politic thing to do, Fitt did not stay in the committee room while Orme was speaking. Instead he want upstairs to the bar and talked to a Swedish journalist.

Meanwhile Faulkner was in his office with Napier discussing the statement which would declare that the Executive had fallen. The announcement would give the voting in the Executive showing that there had been a division of seven to four in favour of phasing the Council of Ireland, but since the decision could not be made unanimous, the government had fallen.

Sittings of the assembly began at half past two and it was Faulkner's intention to make the announcement at that hour. However, it was almost that time and there was therefore not much time to prepare an elaborate statement. Napier persuaded Faulkner against making the statement immediately because there was a slim chance that the SDLP assembly party might change its mind.

For the next twenty minutes the two men discussed how ministers of the Executive should conduct themselves in the assembly if he delayed the announcement. For example, should they enter the chamber to answer questions during question time and take part in other business? Napier was urging Faulkner to leave the statement to the end of the sitting and then reveal what happened, but Faulkner was unhappy about this.

The Stormont grapevine, the most vigorous of plants, was already indicating that the Executive had fallen. Partly to allay such fears, Napier headed off towards the front benches at a quarter to three. On his way he met a smiling Harry West who taunted that the Executive had fallen. Napier said nothing and went into the chamber.

Fitt was still upstairs in the bar. Somewhat later, and for no reason that he could recall, he left his drink and went into the corridor, at the end of which he caught sight of Faulkner's heels disappearing. Fitt knew instantly that the Chief Minister was on his way to the chamber to make the announcement. Fitt ran after him and breathlessly managed to stop him short of the chamber door. Faulkner showed Fitt the short statement which would end the Executive.

Fitt pleaded with Faulkner not to make the statement. He did not know what was happening at his party meeting with Orme but he was willing to gamble on the outcome. Faulkner was worried about delaying the statement any further since he saw little hope of change. After all, the SDLP had taken two votes on the matter.

But Fitt was persistent and in the end managed to turn a reluctant Faulkner away from the door. No fiction writer could have cut the margin any finer. Faulkner returned to his room after promising Fitt one hour's delay. Fitt then went to the committee room where the SDLP was meeting Orme.

When he arrived, Orme had just finished speaking. He had spelt out in detail what he thought the consequences would be if the SDLP brought the Executive down at this critical time. Orme was taken by Fitt to Faulkner's room and Fitt then joined his party meeting.

John Hume re-entered at roughly the same time. Hume had already phoned a civil servant in Dublin to say that the Executive had fallen. In fact, Dublin had received a flurry of phone calls in the same vein. Orme had spoken to the Republic's Foreign Minister, Dr Garret FitzGerald, and Faulkner had phoned the Republic's Prime Minister, Liam Cosgrave and the opposition leader, Jack Lynch. It was beginning to leak to the outside world that the Executive had fallen and this was one of the reasons why Faulkner was worrying about the delay in the formal announcement.

In the SDLP there had been a very heated discussion. Orme's contribution had been to say that if the Executive fell there would be chaos and the SDLP would be blamed. His very presence in that committee room had been a statement to the backbenchers that it was indeed a moment of crisis, and in that, their party leaders had been correct. Another vote was taken. This time it was fourteen votes to five in favour of phasing. And this time, Paddy Devlin voted for phasing.

Fitt raced out of the room to Faulkner's room where the two men once again pumped each other's hands in yet another emotional moment. Quickly an original statement which had been prepared after the Executive, minus the SDLP members, had voted was pulled out of the waste paper basket.

Fitt found Napier, put his arm round him and said, 'We're back in business.' The Alliance leader's reaction was one of immense relief. He had been brooding on the consequences of the Executive breaking up on the sectarian line of weakness. Napier went back to Faulkner's room and told him he would go to the chamber and prepare the way.

The business of government and politics must go on, even when one gets in the way of the other. Everyone by now believed that the Executive was falling and yet the business of the assembly was proceeding as if it were just another day. At three o'clock Paddy Devlin had been asked by Fitt and Major Hall-Thompson, Faulkner's whip, to leave the party meeting and move the estimates of his department as scheduled.

When Napier looked into the chamber he was pleased. He had the task of to creating a gap in the business for Faulkner's statement. The job fortuituously was to be made easy because Lord Dunleath of the Alliance Party, the assistant Speaker, was in the chair and speaking to the estimates was Dr Derek Crothers, another Alliance member. Napier first approached Dunleath, then Dr Crothers. Those watching thought he was preparing the death notice.

Moments later Faulkner entered. Crothers continued for a short time and space was then made for an urgent statement. Faulkner rose to a hushed chamber.

'I appreciate the indulgence of the House,' Faulkner began. 'I regard the statement I have to make a particularly important one—perhaps the most important one that has ever been made in this assembly or in the parliament that was here before that.'

In a long statement Faulkner then outlined areas of commerce, agriculture and environment which would be co-ordinated by a Council of Ministers. It was apparent to those who knew what was in the original Sunningdale communique that the Council would now have no executive role and no cross-border parliamentary tier in the first phase.

If the Executive had survived the UWC strike, the amended Sunningdale agreement would have provided a more stable basis for the power-sharing government. In due course the 1977–8 assembly election might have confirmed the constitutional arrangement and allowed a full Council of Ireland to come into being eventually. This was the process the loyalists feared—a slow maturing of power sharing into a peaceful establishment of a Council of Ireland opening the door to peaceful and agreed reunification one day.

If the phasing had been managed earlier, or been part of the original Sunningdale agreement, then the UWC strike might never have occurred. On the other hand, there can be no doubt that the phasing was only made possible by the February general election results in Northern Ireland and the consequent UWC strike, for without the strike the sub-committee negotiations might have dragged on for months. Without the strike, Rees and the British government might not have become so impatient about the phasing negotiations.

But the question must be asked: without the UWC strike would the SDLP rank and file finally have agreed to the phasing? Probably not, because the Council of Ireland, along with power sharing, was a main price of SDLP participation in the administration of Northern Ireland, a political entity they believed in their hearts should not exist.

It is perfectly possible therefore to conclude that the UWC strike did not shorten the life of the power-sharing Executive. Quite the contrary. It prolonged it!

* *

The rumours that the Executive had fallen had reached Hawthornden Road and there was premature rejoicing. When the statement about the phasing of Sunningdale became public, there was deep disappointment and not a little wonderment about the magic that had saved the Executive.

The events did have the effect of clarifying for the UWC what its aim should be. Their one expressed aim had been a fresh election to the assembly but members of the co-ordinating committee began to realise that if the Executive fell, it might take everything else with it. The Rev. Ian Paisley said, 'The Executive will not last for four years. The majority of people in Northern Ireland will bring it down by refusing to acknowledge it and refusing to co-operate in any way.

'The strike must now continue until negotiations are opened up with Her Majesty's Government concerning the Constitution Act, the Sunningdale agreement and new elections for the assembly.'

The loyalists were unwilling to acknowledge how much damage had been done to the original Council of Ireland proposals. Much nationalist opinion was against the new agreement.

The Falls Road branch of the SDLP that night, Wednesday 22 May, totally rejected the modification and called for a full meeting of the party.

The Irish Prime Minister, Liam Cosgrave, accepted the situation reluctantly, saying to the Dáil that he would have preferred all aspects of Sunningdale to stand. 'The maintenance and development of the Executive are especially vital to the interests of the minority in Northern Ireland, who through it, have for the first time in the history of Northern Ireland, secured full and fair representation in government.' He was saying in effect that power sharing was more important than the Council of Ireland for the time being.

Jack Lynch, opposition leader and leader of the Fianna Fáil Party which had a strong republican tradition, and unfettered with the same responsibilities of statesmanship, was less happy. He said the second phase of the Council of Ireland, which would involve all its meaningful aspects, was dependent on the outcome of an election in the North in four years' time. There was, he said, an inference that the British government was not maintaining its powers under the Sunningdale agreement and was giving them instead to the electoral will of a small part of Ireland.

There was a strong feeling in Dublin that, in allowing the phasing while at the same time failing to take effective action against the UWC strike, the British government was renouncing an agreement to which it had been party. There was, however, a realisation that if Catholics and Protestants, partitionists and anti-partitionists, came to an agreement, then the Republic of Ireland would have to swallow it.

With that Faulkner had achieved more in relation to Northern Ireland's most basic problem than any Unionist politician since the establishment of Northern Ireland. He had done so by attracting the trust of mainstream Catholic politicians and, in turn, trusting them. When one considers that his background was steeped in Unionist orthodoxy, his position was remarkable.

* *

When the back-slapping and emotion of the event had died down Faulkner found that the phasing brought relief from pressure within his own party, but only an easing. The chairman of the Faulknerite backbench committee pronounced that the phasing seemed the proper way to proceed for the next three years.

And the UWC, after the initial disappointment, drew strength from the realisation that the Executive was becoming vulnerable. As Harry Murray put it that Wednesday night, 'You will not crack the British government because they can't afford to give in. There's only one way and that is through the Executive.'

By now the strikers had begun to issue passes to allow certain categories of people through the barricades. This posed a greater threat to the government than simple barricades which could be represented as riotous behaviour. Barricades associated with codified passes were something else. The UWC announced that anyone who wanted to travel without hindrance must have a valid UWC pass. The house in Hawthornden was besieged by applicants, an embarrassing proportion of whom were business and professional men who generally remained aloof from anything connected with paramilitary activity.

Parking near the UWC became difficult, so long were the queues for passes. Every minute that this continued brought into sharp contrast the images of government seemingly incapable of controlling movement in its own back yard. The UWC control may have lacked sophistication but it was no less effective for that. It even prompted the rise of a special kind of humour. Harry Murray himself was chief among the vetting committee.

I was doing some interviews with people asking for special passes. One character came in with a lorry loaded with racing pigeons and said he was going to Beleek but he didn't have enough fuel. . . . I told him his pigeons could walk to Beleek and fly back.

Two chaps came in from the Shorts aircraft factory. One was a security guard with dogs to look after; the other was a manager responsible for a boiler. The guard said he wanted to travel to feed the dogs and, since he supported us one hundred per cent, he would not be travelling at all if it hadn't been for the dogs, so I gave him a pass.

The other man said he was in charge of a boiler worth £6,000. He said if it wasn't fed it could cool too quickly and blow up. I said, 'Not granted'.

He said, 'But you gave passes for a couple of old dogs.' And I said, 'I could eat the dogs but I couldn't eat a boiler.'

A man behind in the queue was listening to the refusals and started shouting that I was a bloody dictator and Cromwell had nothing on me.

'I'll tell you, mate,' said I, 'you have no hope of a pass.'

Murray was unaware at that time that he was not the only source of UWC passes. The government began forging the passes on a large scale, printing them in Belfast. The trick was eventually discovered by the strikers, hence there were three different issues of passes during the strike.

Murray and others in the UWC previously unconnected with paramilitary-backed activity were at times amazed at the power they were wielding. Sometimes they stumbled by accident on ways of extending it. A good example was when the management of Harland and Wolff shipyard telephoned Hawthornden Road to make arrangements for bringing back to port a large ship on sea trials with several hundred workers on board. It had sailed before the stoppage and found on its return that Belfast was practically at a standstill. Tugs were needed to berth the ship.

Until then Murray had not given any thought to the importance of tugs. When Harland and Wolff put one of the tug captains on the line, Murray told him that the ship could be brought in but that nothing else was to be assisted in or out of the port except in the case of fire.

'You're joking,' said the captain.

'No, I'm not,' Murray replied. 'and you can thank Harland and Wolff for putting that idea in my head.'

As Murray said afterwards, 'It was just a matter of giving orders and people accepted them. Nobody seemed to question them and that annoyed me at times. Nobody said, "Who are you?" If they had, a lot might not have happened.'

Perhaps. But the man in the queue who had called him a dictator worse than Cromwell had been refused a pass.

ELEVEN

On another front events were happening very fast. The ban on the transport of petrol and oil, imposed on the Tuesday, 21 May, was by now biting deeply.

By Wednesday there were long queues at filling stations and they were being overwhelmed. The stations began imposing a ration of one or two pounds' worth of fuel. The situation became chaotic very rapidly because the oil companies had already been restricting supplies due to the hijacking of their road tankers. So when the specific ban on tanker movements was imposed by the UWC, stocks were already low in many filling stations.

Behind the scenes the Oil Industry Emergency Committee (OIEC) had convened to deal with the crisis. Membership consisted mainly of representatives of the big oil companies operating in Northern Ireland: Shell Mex, BP, Esso, Burmah, Texaco, Mobil, Gulf and Paktank, a company renting storage tanks to other companies such as Conoco, Jet, ICI Chemicals and Burmah. The manager of the Shell refinery (the only one in the province), Alison Lennox, was automatically chairman since he was responsible for the largest storage capacity, was the only producer and supplied about sixty per cent of the local market.

The OIEC had a contingency plan for a republican uprising but not for a loyalist one in which their own shop stewards very suddenly became the managers. The OIEC had issued the companies with lists of approved customers, but, with the usual shambles, different companies were being given different lists. Confusion reigned. The OIEC knew that official policy was not to negotiate with the UWC but in the end the committee had no choice. Government in the guise of the Department of Commerce could offer little help.

A three-man OIEC delegation turned up at Hawthornden Road and was mildly surprised at its reception. Alison Lennox introduced himself and Glen Barr stepped forward and did the same.

The oilmen found that the UWC listened to them courteously and treated their point of view sympathetically.

The UWC and the OIEC were agreed on most of the list of essential users. Some on the OIEC list had not been thought of by the UWC, such as undertakers who needed petrol for their hearses and oil for their furnaces. At this stage the UWC was unsure what status to grant domestic gas plants throughout the province. Northern Ireland did not have a natural gas grid and gas plants were dependent on naphtha produced in the Belfast refinery and transported by tanker everywhere except Belfast, which was supplied by pipeline.

The two committees clashed on one important essential user. High on the OIEC list and deliberately omitted from the UWC one were the army, police and other sections of the security forces. Lennox pointed out an inconsistency in the UWC position, which was that it was claiming that the strike was non-violent, but was laying itself open to charges of stimulating violence because the police were not mobile. 'You could be doing the IRA's job for them. You have brought the province to a standstill and they have never been able to do this.'

Barr changed the subject but this was the high point of hostilities between them, and the rest of the meeting passed off in a relatively calm atmosphere. Most of the room believed that oil would not be the target of government reaction. Electricity was more likely.

They were wrong. Oil was indeed the factor which eventually provoked the army into direct strike-breaking action, thereby bringing the situation to a head.

****

Now that the phasing agreement was out of the way the Executive could at long last direct its full attention to the stoppage. On Thursday 23 May John Hume unfolded the oil plan—the first major offensive by government. The document read as follows:

Plan for the Department of Commerce to take over, control and distribute petroleum products and LPG (liquid petroleum gas) to essential users

1. There already exists an oil contingency plan produced in 1972 for the distribution of petroleum products to essential users. Present circumstances necessitate the

revision of this plan to ensure the take-over, control and distribution of these products. The following 'revised' plan has been produced by the Department in consultation with the Government Emergency Committee, the army and the Oil Industry Emergency Committee.

2. Under existing powers the Department of Commerce will requisition such land, property, plant, vehicles and products in the Harbour Estate, in the refinery, the LPG plant and the petroleum operation as may be considered necessary.

3. The products already in storage, being sufficient to supply normal demand for fourteen days, will meet the needs of essential users for a much greater period.

4. The army will mount guard over the whole area and its installations.

5. The petroleum distributers will be invited to operate the plant and distribute on behalf of the Department of Commerce. (The workers have been loyal to their companies.) If they refuse or cannot do so, the army on behalf of the Department will put in technical personnel to operate the plant and distribute by tanker throughout Northern Ireland using army drivers and guards. Certain government officials to administer distribution may be required.

6. Compensation will have to be paid to the companies concerned.

7. Distribution of the products will be through two channels.
    i. Direct to essential bulk users, e.g. hospitals, medical and welfare services, food processing, water and sewage.
    ii. Twenty-one garages distributed evenly throughout the province whose premises, product and equipment will be requisitioned by the Department. These garages have already been identified and have been cleared by the army who will mount guard on them at all times. The operation of the garages will be done on behalf of the Department by the occupiers or by government personnel.

8. Approximately 6,500 essential users have already been identified by departments and special coupons for their use are held by the Department of Commerce. In the absence of reliable postal services, distribution of these

coupons will be made by departments by whatever means they consider necessary. A system of licensing for other persons needing petrol for emergencies will be instituted and operated from government offices evenly distributed across the country.

9. The army recommend that the Department also requisition the oil distribution centre at Londonderry for ease of distribution in that area. The procedure will be the same.

10. There are oil depots at Larne, Carrickfergus as well as Londonderry, which will not be requisitioned and who will have product in storage. Garages will have some supplies in store. It is envisaged that these will continue to operate so long as supplies last or additional supplies can be legally brought in. This plan is designed to safeguard a sufficient quantity of products to ensure a continued distribution to essential users over an extended period; the plan is not designed to prevent the law-abiding citizens getting lawful supplies. A maximum price order exists to prevent exploitation.

11. The GOC (General Officer Commanding) has stated that if the political decision is taken to implement the plan the tasks assigned to his forces are feasible provided:
    i. The necessary troops are made available from Great Britain
    ii. The legal implications are examined
    iii. The possibility of sabotage is considered.

12. It would be wise to work on the assumption that the staff of the oil companies would not be willing to work and that technical army staff would be needed. A period of two or three days would be needed after the political decision had been taken to mount this exercise.

13. The Chief Legal Advisor of the Department of Legal Affairs has advised that the proposals are within our powers and he is now working out the necessary details.

14. The identification of the installations at the Harbour Estate and the twenty-one garages as government-controlled points of distribution will expose these places to risk of attack. Indeed the identification of essential users (for they will very soon be seen to be the only people receiving government supplies) may expose them to intimidation. These possibilities are, however, inherent in the plan. A more

worrying aspect is the fact that the Belfast gas manufacturing plant is situated within the area to be requisitioned, but will not itself be requisitioned. Workers may refuse to pass through army lines to get to work, thus endangering the supplies of gas to Belfast and other towns in North Down. A consequential move on oil therefore may be to requisition simultaneously the gas works. A further consequence to a move under this plan on oil distribution may be the complete withdrawal of all labour from the power stations.

The paragraph outlining the views of the general in command of the army in Northern Ireland is revealing. Clearly he did not have enough men for the plan. The combination of action against both Protestant and Catholic paramilitaries was using all his present resources.

His worries about the Executive not having the legal framework in place could have arisen from the fact that the army had in the past been acting illegally in Northern Ireland in the matter of powers of arrest. This had been exposed through the courts in a case, poignantly enough, involving John Hume. Parliament at Westminster had been forced to rush a bill through both Commons and Lords conferring retrospective legality, an embarrassing episode for the army, and for politicians who had not done their homework.

The GOC's concern about sabotage by loyalist paramilitaries arose on two counts: he believed that once the army began running a service, it might automatically become the target for such actions. The UWC was constantly urging the army to take over services abandoned or restricted, but the army may have exaggerated the sabotage threat in this particular respect. The UWC wanted army effort tied up; its game plan did not involve sabotage of largely Protestant-run services and utilities.

However, the authorities, including the army, believed that there was a real danger of sabotage at the refinery and storage tanks if the loyalist paramilitaries got wind of the oil plan during the two or three days needed between the political decision and implementation. Sabotage of these installations could be prevented after occupation. In behind these fears was a nagging worry that there were security leaks from both the Executive and Northern Ireland Civil Service.

A very uncomfortable implication of the plan perhaps lay in its final sentence which stated that the move on oil might precipitate a total electricity blackout. Everyone involved at Stormont knew that the army could not run the power system.

As the oil plan was being prepared, the Electricity Service gloomily announced that the generators would have to shut down at Ballylumford in three or four days' time because of a lack of hydrogen for cooling, and other essential chemicals. However, the UWC then allowed the materials to travel by tanker from Belfast to sustain the meagre thirty per cent supply. It was just another noose round the neck of electricity supply which the UWC could tighten as it wished.

John Hume had praised his Northern Ireland Electricity Service in public but in private he had been having crisis meetings with its management. Hume had an electricity plan and the electricity people did not like it.

As a Derry man, Hume knew something of the circumstances of the Coolkeeragh power station just outside the city. By Thursday 23 May its main generating sets, capable of producing 360 megawatts, lay idle. A small gas turbine generator was giving 60 megawatts. Reports reaching Hume's Department of Commerce through official channels said the big generators were silent because the workers were refusing to operate them, but Hume's private lines of communication were saying otherwise. Approximately forty per cent of the Coolkeeragh workers were Catholic and not part of the loyalist stoppage. The Catholic power workers told Hume that if he made it possible, they could run Coolkeeragh themselves at full power for a limited period.

This was the basis of Hume's plan. He wanted to split the distribution grid into two sections, run Coolkeeragh at full power for the north west and use this energy to put industry in that area back to work. Hume's aim was to demonstrate that the stoppage was affecting only the Protestant part of the province. He wanted to demonstrate that the essential character of the stoppage was compulsory lock-out, not voluntary strike action.

So Hume told the Electricity Service to implement this plan and allow Coolkeeragh back on full power serving only Derry and the north west. But the electricity managers refused. A battle of wills ensued.

The Northern Ireland Electricity Service (NIES) said that while the Minister of Commerce had a general responsibility for maintaining electricity supplies, he was not empowered to interfere in the day-to-day running of the service and to issue detailed instructions. Hume then took legal advice, on the back of which he issued instructions that the Catholic workers of Coolkeeragh should be given the chance to run the station.

The NIES countered that although Catholic workers accounted for almost half the workforce, Catholics were not evenly distributed among the jobs in each shift essential to running the machines. A skeleton workforce might just manage by doubling up and by ignoring union-management agreements. Hume pointed out that a State of Emergency existed and, in any case, the trade union movement had promised backing for any moves necessary to get people back to work.

The NIES moved position. It said that if Colkeeragh opened up with full power, the Protestant workers still producing at the other big power station at Larne, Ballylumford, would walk out. This would mean half the system would be lost immediately without an adequate guarantee that Coolkeeragh would be able to do what the Minister wanted. What, for example, would happen if Coolkeeragh's Protestant workers demanded that they return to work? There was a danger of sabotage.

Hume's attitude was that the UWC was simply playing about with Ballylumford anyway, repeatedly bringing it to the brink of a complete halt, and then retreating at the last minute.

None of this passed the lips of the NIES public spokesman, Hugo Patterson, who became a household name during the stoppage. Patterson began each day by phoning for instruction the NIES engineering director, who believed the public should be told as much as possible. Patterson then went to the BBC radio studios (the BBC had the only local radio at that time) where he issued his news, usually so bad that he was known as 'Mr Doomsday' by his listeners in the UWC. But the long periods without power were sufficient in themselves to convince Hugo Patterson's large audience that he could not be crying 'wolf'. As one Belfast journalist put it, 'Hugo Patterson's revelations that we were "tittering, tottering, teetering" on the brink left me tittering and tottering down the stairs as I tried to face another day.'

UWC brinkmanship with the electricity supplies had angered Hume almost to the point of wishing the Ballylumford workers would just leave and be done with it. It would be easier for service personnel to enter an unmanned power station. By this time the UK government was beginning to explore the option of putting Royal Navy engineers into the power stations. The navy had experience of running small shore-based electricity systems abroad.

In resisting Hume, the NIES was in its own terms protecting a very valuable aspect of its operation: the absence of sectarian disruption experienced by other big concerns from time to time. Even at the height of the UWC stoppage, Catholics were being allowed through UDA barricades to Ballylumford to work alongside Protestants if their job was considered necessary. The technical staff and engineers were of mixed religion and their efforts to keep the system running at between twenty-five and thirty per cent of normal power were outstanding. Engineers from other parts of the world came to study how they had done it. The management believed that if the Catholic part of the workforce were used to try to break the strike, the cohesion of the workforce would have been shattered for years to come.

The NIES technical director was Jim Smith, who found himself having to define the role of an electrical supply undertaking functioning in a society which was split down the middle. He had constantly to examine critically his own motivation because, in defying his political master, he was ploughing a lone furrow. He believed that his role was to supply electricity for as long as he could with the resources available, to as many people as possible, and to resist pressure to do otherwise, except for genuine technical reasons. He believed that the status of chartered engineer explicitly reinforced this view of how he should conduct himself.

He was fighting hard to keep himself outside the political arena. Nevertheless he went to Coolkeeragh himself to put the issues to the Catholic workers. He told them that if they managed to run the station without Protestants, there was a strong possibility that Ballylumford would be abandoned and then taken over by armed service personnel. (He did not say which armed service. Nor did he make known that the security personnel could not operate the station.) His final question to them therefore was whether or not they would work alongside British servicemen—an emotively charged question for them.

At the time they said they would, but later the Coolkeeragh manager reported to Smith that the Provisional IRA had told the men that if they worked in co-operation with British servicemen they might attract IRA retaliation.

The final hurdle for Hume's plan came from the control engineers at Coolkeeragh who said they would operate only according to their employment agreement. In other words, they would continue to direct power from the station as long as there was no shortage of essential workers. A shift consisting of Catholics alone could not meet that condition.

The tussle between Hume and the NIES management continued right to the end. However, the Northern Ireland grid *was* divided into two halves by splitting the 110Kv lines at Dungannon and Ballymena on Tuesday 21 May, but not as part of Hume's plan. The split was an engineering requirement for safety. The amount of current on the transmission lines had dropped so low that there was a danger of automatic trip devices not working to switch off the current if, for example, a power line fell to the ground. Splitting the grid doubled the fault sensing levels.

On Thursday 23 May Derry ran out of domestic gas because naphtha from the Belfast refinery had been stopped by the UWC. Hume believed that this was a purely sectarian move. Derry was his patch. Its plight directed his attention back to his oil plan. However, the involvement of more British troops which would be used directly to break the strike was worrying the Cabinet in London.

TWELVE

So far the British Cabinet had left the tiller to the Northern Ireland Office and the Executive in Belfast. There is evidence that in a manner of speaking, the Cabinet had been testing the resolve of the Executive on a strategy that if the Executive survived, it would deserve support; if it cracked, it would have broken anyway. Rees had been despairing of the Executive ever reaching agreement about the Council of Ireland, and his belief that this issue might in the end collapse the Executive had been communicated to Cabinet colleagues weeks before.

The phasing agreement meant that, in the eyes of the Cabinet, the Executive had won its spurs and earned a greater measure of support. Members of the Executive suspected that this might have been the case and never really forgave the Cabinet for not putting its full weight behind them right from the start.

When the Executive met on Thursday 23 May it was in a bellicose mood. That day a joint British and Irish Law Commission report was published. The Commission had been set up as part of the Sunningdale settlement to look into the problems of extraditing terrorists who fled over the border between Northern Ireland and the Republic. The Unionists wanted extradition for politically motivated crime; the Republic wanted all-Ireland extra-territorial courts.

The Commission's report pleased no one by recommending a system whereby the existing courts in both parts of Ireland could try certain crimes, irrespective of where they were committed on the island.

So Faulkner now found that pressure from his own supporters, just reduced by the Sunningdale phasing agreement, was now renewed on this question of law reform. It had leaked that the Commission had split along national lines on the extradition question. The Faulkner Unionists believed the same as the loyalists: that the Irish government was making no concession to help power sharing in the north. Relationships with Dublin were cooling. The Irish Prime Minister and members of his Cabinet saw the British Ambassador in Dublin to say that a combination of delays in ratifying Sunningdale and inaction against the loyalist strikers was responsible for escalating the present crisis. In private, the ruling Fine Gael Party in Dublin felt much the same as the opposition Fianna Fáil, which was that there was precious little of the Sunningdale agreement left.

But if the phasing agreement and other factors were pushing Dublin a little further away, this was welcome to the Faulkner Unionists. However, they were inclined to agree with Dublin that London had not been nearly forceful enough in tackling the strike. The Executive now had before it a plan of action, the oil plan, which would force the army away from its preferred position of spectator. Now it was the Executive's turn to present an ultimatum. The plan was given to the Northern Ireland Office with the message that if the British government did not take the decision to proceed with it, every member of the Executive would resign inside twenty-four hours.

Some members were worrying about the position of Roy Bradford within the Executive. The GOC had pointedly made clear that unity of purpose was vital. Bradford continued to be strongly in favour of opening lines of communication with the UWC and was now strongly opposed to the use of troops. His thinking paralleled that of the electricity service; he thought the action would demolish more essential services than it would save.

Though now politically isolated, Bradford's position was echoed elsewhere. Among the higher levels of command in the army there was concern about whether the army had sufficient manpower to cope if the UWC ordered a withdrawal from nearly every essential service. To see the way the sums worked, it had been estimated that to open the roads in Protestant east Belfast 3,000 troops were needed. Round the clock presence to keep them open would necessitate three shifts, meaning 9,000 men altogether. In other words over half the army in Northern Ireland would be needed to keep only a portion of Belfast free from barricades. All that before serving the need to provide essential services and to guard vital installations throughout the province— and evidence that in the first place, 3,000 soldiers had had only limited success under the doctrine of limited force.

Finally there was a political limitation in Bradford's view. He believed that one of the central lessons of the past five years was that the army was not capable of imposing a military solution in relation to the IRA. As he said, 'Surely hardliners like myself who had to learn the hard way that there was no military solution were not going to have to unlearn the lesson the hard way.'

These views hardly endeared him to his Executive colleagues and they suspected him of passing information about tactics to the UWC. In particular, he was accused of passing details of the oil plan and its twenty-three filling stations to be taken over. The very next day after the plan had been revealed to the Executive, the UWC began taking over filling stations—and Bradford was blamed. Bradford had openly visited the UDA headquarters in east Belfast ten days before the Executive fell.

Furthermore, on Friday 17 May and on Wednesday 22 May the commanders of the UDA and the UVF in east Belfast visited Bradford's home outside Bangor, about twelve miles from the city. Bradford declared that both men were his constituents and this was the basis of the meetings. He was adamant that he confined his conversation to a discussion of attitudes on both sides and denied that he even knew many of the detailed plans. Details had not been discussed in front of him by other Executive members because they distrusted him, he said.

After the Executive meeting that Thursday, Austin Currie and some other Executive members found they did not have enough petrol in their official cars to get home. The Northern Ireland Office was landed with the responsibility of finding cans to fill their tanks. A piece of symbolism. That night Frank Cooper of the Northern Ireland Office telephoned Faulkner and Oliver Napier and asked them to meet the Prime Minister, Harold Wilson, and other senior Cabinet ministers at Chequers in Buckinghamshire the following day, Friday.

At long last, something was happening.

* *

Napier was at Stormont on Friday morning, 24 May, as requested. He was met by Kenneth Bloomfield, secretary to the Executive and Tom Roberts, a senior Northern Ireland government information advisor. All three went by army helicopter to RAF Aldergrove at Belfast airport, about fifteen miles away, where Brian Faulkner was already waiting. The group then boarded a plane for RAF Northolt outside London on the A40.

On their arrival at Chequers they were greeted by Harold Wilson. Gerry Fitt, who had been in London for a Commons debate, had arrived just before them. Before lunch there was a an hour-long debate in an upstairs room. The Executive leaders were faced by a high-powered Cabinet committee. Alongside Wilson were the Defence Secretary, Roy Mason, the Attorney General, Samuel Silkin and of course, Merlyn Rees. Wilson dominated the meeting and began by spelling out the limits beyond which the government would not go.

This was not what the Executive leaders wanted to hear. They wanted the answer to a very basic question: would the British government fight the strikers?

Discussions broke off for lunch downstairs in the elegant dining room with its long thin table and walls covered with paintings. The topic of conversation was still the crisis, but the level of interchange was now informal.

Then upstairs for another two hours of meeting. It was becoming clear that the purpose was to furnish senior Cabinet members with an impression of the Executive's resolve before committing resources. Faulkner, Fitt and Napier were at Chequers to have questions put to them, not to have their questions answered. The Northern Ireland ministers must have had made a favourable impression because the Prime Minister indicated that troops would be moved to guarantee essential services. However, it was made clear once again that service personnel could not operate the electrical power system on their own. While they might move to help safeguard power they would need the help of civilian workers to keep electricity flowing. To begin with therefore, the troops would be used to unblock oil and petrol.

The feeling among the three Executive leaders as they flew back to Aldergrove was one of disappointment. They were returning with vague promises. They had no defined picture in their minds of exactly what the British government would do next. Napier still believed that the battle should be fought in the power stations and viewed soldiers in filling stations as second best. His outlook was coloured in part because his five-week-old baby was very ill. Its bottles could be sterilised only with difficulty because the Napier house was without electricity.

A Cabinet meeting was called that evening in Downing Street and Rees had promised Faulkner that he would phone with the decision on the oil plan. The call was put through to

Faulkner's home in the Co. Down countryside at about eleven o'clock in the evening. It was an open unscrambled line so Rees simply said that a decision had been taken that he would firmly support. Faulkner then knew that the Cabinet had decided to implement the oil plan. A similar call reached Fitt at his London hotel and he too phoned Faulkner. Both now expected that a move would be made no later than Sunday morning, notwithstanding the fact that the GOC had stated within the plan itself that he would need more time.

The UWC was moving rather faster on oil. Two shop stewards representing the oil industry went to Hawthornden Road and on a large map plotted a filling station approximately every nine miles to which petrol would be supplied under UWC auspices. They included garages in Catholic areas and they took care to choose garages belonging to different companies on a repeating pattern. The oil shop stewards were given a free hand in this exercise. The co-ordinating committee was beginning to act like a government, making policy decisions and leaving the executive action and the detail to 'civil servants'. They used the same administrative system to regulate the supply of animal feedstuff.

The UWC filling stations were not meant to supply the ordinary public, only the needs of the paramilitary organisations. A secondary function was to supply people issued with UWC passes for essential services. Every person who drew up at a UWC pump was vetted and asked for their UWC pass. Many were turned away by the UWC 'inspector'. One garage was near a main hospital, the Royal Victoria. The 'inspector' was allowing petrol to some of those with hospital car park stickers on their windscreens, but not all. Seeing a sticker on a the windscreen, the 'inspector' asked, 'Are you a doctor or a nurse?'

'I'm a consultant.'

'Sorry, doctors and nurses only.'

In their own terms, the UWC operation in the filling stations was successful. Up until Sunday evening the UWC claimed to have supplied 142 stations. With UWC approval, the Belfast refinery had 120 tankers on the road supplying these stations between Friday 24 May and the evening of Sunday 26 May. This was a level of activity not far short of what the Oil Industry Emergency Committee estimated would be needed to supply its own list of essential users.

It meant that the UWC had finally established control over all forms of energy, over transport, farming and commerce. It could be argued that it was limiting the scope of the security forces. Confrontation in these circumstances with the lawful authority of government seemed inevitable, but a final effort to avoid this was in train.

The deputation voted into being at the meeting of 'moderates' at the Quaker Meeting House in Belfast the previous Tuesday evening had been active. Its members had travelled to London and straight to the House of Commons, where they were nonplussed at the ill-informed attitudes they were uncovering. There was a cross-party feeling at Westminster of total exasperation with the province and evidence of patience wearing thin. Their most significant meeting was with the Labour Party's Northern Ireland Committee which included Kevin MacNamara and Jock Stollard. It was an experience which one of the delegation described as 'shattering'.

Sandy Scott, the prominent shipyard trade unionist, felt assured of at least a polite hearing if only because he had in the past done work for the Northern Ireland Labour Committee in Belfast. However, it was agreed that when they entered the room, Professor Alan Milne, notwithstanding his blindness, would act as leading spokesman. It went very badly from the beginning. Professor Milne's distinction between 'talks' and 'negotiation' could not be perceived by those across the table, as Scott made clear.

> Suddenly MacNamara became very emotional and shook with rage. He said the was not going to sit at the table and listen to any more of what they were saying. He was not going to talk with bully boys and thugs. The delegation could wait until the sewage came up through the streets before he would do so. He thumped the table in front of him, closed his briefcase and walked out shouting with rage. Then Nonie McClure became emotional herself and ran after him. She said, 'Mr MacNamara, you are not going to talk to these people like that. I'm a Catholic and a civil righter.'

Scott then joined the pair who by that time were in the corridor. He tried talking to MacNamara calmly, saying that they were not intending to cause offence. He said they were part of the democratic process, that they were making representation.

MacNamara returned to the room but the damage had been done. The nature of the delegation was not understood; the all-pervading attitude in London was that any group, no matter how broadly based, which sought lines of communication with the UWC must be a mouthpiece of the loyalist paramilitaries and speaking treason.

The delegation also saw among others, Ron Hayward, secretary to the Labour Party, whom they found much more open-minded and helpful. Jeremy Thorpe, leader of the Liberals, also seemed to see force in their arguments. He helped by promising to use his influence to secure a meeting with Wilson or Rees, but the prospect was not hopeful since they were both at Chequers. It was in fact Hayward who made a meeting possible. It was arranged that Scott would stay by the telephone at his hotel in case there was any news.

By this time the delegation was demoralised. It had the impression that there was little understanding of what was happening and why it was happening in Ulster, compounded by a doubt that its action was too late. Scott himself was exhausted and had gone to bed early when, at a quarter to nine, the telephone rang to say that Rees would meet them in fifteen minutes time at the Treasury.

Scott tried to contact the delegation members but many had felt so pessimistic about making any headway that they had scattered. Some had left for home. In the time available, Scott could only reach two clergymen, the Rev. John Stewart of the Northern Ireland Labour Party and the Rev. Derek McKelvie of the Northern Ireland Council of Social Service.

Rees told them he could spare only a quarter of an hour since he was about to fly back to Northern Ireland. He had just come from the Cabinet meeting only yards away where the decision had been taken to implement the oil plan. So for the first time, Rees began to listen to people who were able to articulate loyalist concerns conveyed in a manner and within a context which posed no political threat to him. These men were not supporters of the UWC or paramilitary organisations. What they were saying interested him greatly, for he delayed the helicopter waiting to take him to the plane and remained with them for an hour. As Scott recalled:

We exceeded our brief by talking about class consciousness and told him he must do nothing that would drive the UWC into a more extreme position. If he opened up a dialogue he could channel them into more constructive lines. We pointed out that the very things government were doing to protect and maintain the Executive would eventually destroy not only the Executive but the whole concept of power sharing.

We told him that it looked to us as if the upholding of the individuals who made up the Executive was regarded as more important than the principle of power sharing. Furthermore, the government's public relations had been disastrous. . . . Rees agreed that the public relations had been disastrous.

So at the end of the day the perseverance of the delegation had paid off to a limited extent. By the time they saw Rees, the three men had decided to cast aside the device of suggesting talks about taking electricity out of the dispute. What was happening in the power stations was a symptom, not a cause. They got down to the bedrock of Protestant discontent and how the strike was being handled. That was what Rees needed to hear; it was why the helicopter was kept waiting.

Rees had spend much of that day listening to the case as put by the leaders in the Executive. The three men in front of him were telling another truth. They were saying that Faulkner's party could not bear the strains for much longer, that the Faulkner Unionists had lost too much support in Northern Ireland to survive, that the Protestant middle class were getting offside. In his heart Rees must have believed what he was being told. It meant that the phasing of Sunningdale in itself was not going to save the Executive.

But in the short term did this all mean that the troops should not move in support of the Executive? It was pragmatism against principle, and the decision of use the army to implement the oil plan had been made in principle at the highest levels of government in Britain.

THIRTEEN

That same night, Friday 24 May, four people were killed as a result of the strike. Two of the victims were the Catholic owners of a bar situated about five miles south of the Co. Antrim town of Ballymena. They were murdered for opening their business in defiance of the strike.

According to eye-witnesses, two minibuses and a taxi drew up outside the pub from the direction of Ballymena. Men emerged and immediately began to attack the building, breaking the windows. First a broom shaft was thrown through an upstairs window where seven of the pub owner's eight young children were watching television. While the pub was being smashed, raiders burst into the small kitchen at the back and shot dead in cold blood 54-year-old Seán Byrne and his 45-year-old brother, Brendan. Their sister and wives escaped by climbing out of a window.

The murders shocked the province and exposed the evil underbelly of the strike more starkly than before. The attack on the Byrne pub, which was also their home, was not an isolated incident that night. In Ballymena itself, a gang wrecked three pubs and a snack bar which had opened for business. In Ballymoney to the north, men in two minibuses toured pubs and ordered customers out.

In Co. Tyrone, on the main Dungannon to Omagh Road, 29-year-old Patrick McGirr and 20-year-old Eileen McCrory were killed when their car smashed into a tree deliberately felled across the road as a barricade. Two petrol stations in the Belfast area which had been open for business were the targets of bomb attacks. So was a pub in Belfast and another in Portadown.

Thus on Friday night came the first clear signs of sectarian violence from Protestants associated with the strike and at the time it looked like the beginning of a new and very ugly phase. On the morning of Saturday 25 May there was a general air of helplessness. Neither side seemed to be moving and things were going from bad to worse. There were dire warnings from grocers that lack of transport was hitting deliveries and some shops had only a few days' supply of food left. Butchers warned that the long cuts in electricity were reducing refrigeration and new supplies of meat had stopped altogether because the abattoirs were closed.

Newspapers were headlining speculation that at last the army was to be used against the strikers, probably in the oil and petrol sector. It was finally beginning to dawn on elements of the public that perhaps the army could do little to help restore electricity. The clearest indication came from the Electrical Power Engineers Association, which announced that it had told the Prime Minister that if troops entered the power stations its members would leave them. The association was at pains to point out that this would not be action in support of the strike, but because individual engineers feared for their safety. They also made it perfectly clear that if their members abandoned the power stations, the army would be unable to maintain the system and there would be a blackout.

The rump of the delegation which had met Rees returned and spread the word that confrontation was being considered. This hardly needed underlining, since official statements continued to emphasise that there could be no negotiation with self-appointed non-elected bodies. The slim hope of some Protestants that power sharing could survive was evaporating. The gloom deepened as disaffection with the Executive and government spread visibly into farming areas. In north Down and north Londonderry farmers formed long processions of farm machinery and blocked roads.

The ball was clearly in the court of government. It was announced that the Prime Minister would make a ministerial broadcast that evening, to be followed by one from Faulkner. This heightened the expectation that something drastic was about to unfold—an expectation shared by those in Hawthornden Road. In the Commons debate that Thursday, Rees had accused certain Northern Ireland MPs of setting up a provisional government. In a bitter clash Rees said that Rev. Ian Paisley, MP for North Antrim, was dealing with people who wanted to bring down the government of Northern Ireland and were issuing ration books. Paisley challenged Rees to name the people and arrest them.

The UWC noted the exchange and came to the conclusion that arrests might be possible, probably at the time when the Prime Minister was actually broadcasting that evening. They laid plans accordingly. The Hawthornden Road headquarters was to be abandoned by the co-ordinating committee after it had been cleared of all documents. Glen Barr, the chairman, to the detriment of historians, burned his personal record of what had been happening. The UWC members and heads of paramilitary organisations were to re-convene at a community centre in the Ballybeen housing estate in Belfast, where they would watch Wilson on television, electricity supplies permitting.

To safeguard their operation further, three men who were not publicly known and who had lines of communication in the fields of electricity, oil and gas were appointed as second-line commanders. Glen Barr gave them instructions not to come near the co-ordinating committee that night but to remain in touch with each other. They were to keep their radios switched to news broadcasts and if they heard the committee had been arrested, they were to take over.

Before they dispersed for what they thought might be a last time, the co-ordinating committee members issued a statement which they thought would counter what was about to be said by the Prime Minister:

The Ulster Workers' Strike is not an act of rebellion against a lawful authority but a protest within the law against the denial of the democratic rights of the majority of the Ulster people. The loyalty of the majority in Ulster is unchallengeable and their allegiance to Her Majesty the Queen cannot be called into question.

The British government has refused to heed the voice of the majority democratically expressed in the last election. They have imposed on the people a form of government which would not be imposed on any other part of the United Kingdom. This imposition is even contrary to Section 2 of their legislation, the Constitution Act 1973, which requires any Executive to have widespread acceptance in the community.

It was no desire of ours to plunge our beloved province into this strike, but this is the only way we can make our voices heard and our presence felt. Let there be no mistake about it, the Ulster people are determined to win their democratic rights by non-violent means and whether martial law, the arrest of the strike leaders and the army takes over or not, there will be no drawing back until victory is assured.

It seems strange to us that the Prime Minister when in Dublin, sat down with the IRA but he is not prepare to sit down with the working people of Ulster.

And with a sense of impending martyrdom, they scattered until the fateful broadcast. Hawthornden Road, however, was not to be left empty. The loyalist political leaders of the UUUC decided to remain in the hope that if troops made a swoop during the broadcast, they would bag an armoured car full of members of elected representatives. They included an official of the Vanguard Unionist Party, David Trimble, who was a constitutional lawyer at Queen's University in Belfast. The aim was to set a trap to embarrass the government.

If the UWC and loyalist politicians had realised the extent of division among the differing elements of government, they could have saved themselves trouble. Senior members of the Executive spent most of the day, Saturday 25 May, at Stormont. They had turned up confident that the preparations to put the oil plan into effect were being undertaken with all possible haste. However, Rees had returned from London with authority to put the plan into effect whenever he judged was the correct moment and the Executive found that the button had not yet been pushed. Far from it, the oil plan still seemed to be the subject of debate.

The reason soon became clear. The army was very unhappy and was advising Rees not to activate the plan. The army believed that a move on oil could trigger a collapse of the remaining supply of electricity, including sabotage of the transmission lines stretching hundreds of miles across open farmland and virtually impossible to defend. The use of troops in the oil plan might be the signal for Protestant paramilitary organisations to take up arms, first against Catholics, then against soldiers when they intervened. If the activities of the IRA, a small number of people, could tie down 16,000 men as was happening, the argument ran, than a combination of massive civil disobedience and loyalist terrorism could swamp the British army.

For Rees and the British government, even if the Executive had everything going for it otherwise, this was a frightening prospect. So continued army hostility to the plan was the reason for meetings at Stormont that day. The Faulkner Unionists were very worried because they knew that the GOC's concerns were not unreasonable. If conflagration ensued because of deployment of the army, the Faulkner Unionists would be finished politically within the Protestant community. But they were also aware, as were the other two parties of the Executive, that the strike had taken hold because the government had not been firm from the beginning. They were therefore ready to take the chance that showing firmness even at this late hour would re-gain lost ground. Those were the stakes, those were the risks.

For the SDLP the issue had a different perspective. In their view, the final battle to defeat the strike had to be between the army and the loyalist ultras. When the Minister of State, Stanley Orme, had spoken to the SDLP assembly party meeting at Stormont in the drama surrounding the phasing of Sunningdale, he had indicated that in the last resort, the army would challenge the strike.

Now the SDLP found themselves alongside a British establishment divided about using the army. The Cabinet had given its approval and delegated authority to the Northern Ireland Office. The Northern Ireland Office was hesitant. Perhaps Sandy Scott and his two companions had had an effect after all when they had managed to see Rees in London the previous evening. Paddy Devlin was now so angry about the vacillation over implementing the oil plan that he was once again ready to submit his resignation. He was prevailed upon not to because the SDLP would resign en bloc on the issue if necessary. In the end all the Executive left for home not knowing if the oil plan was to be implemented.

Everyone waited for the Prime Minister's broadcast. The UWC was at the Ballybeen housing estate, the loyalist politicians at Hawthornden Road. David Trimble watched the UWC leave with his reference book, Heuston's *Essays on Constitutional Law*, which contained a good essay on martial law.

The whole province waited for Harold Wilson's words. Many were listening on portable radios because power was not available to run television sets. In Derry, television screens faded only minutes before Wilson began.

Harold Wilson began. His words spelt disaster for the Executive.

As the holiday begins, Northern Ireland faces the greatest crisis in her history. It is a crisis equally for all of us who live on this side of the water. What we are seeing in Northern Ireland is not just an industrial strike. It has nothing to do with wages. It has nothing to do with jobs—except to imperil jobs.

It is a deliberate and calculated attempt to use every undemocratic and unparliamentary means for the purpose of bringing down the whole constitution of Northern Ireland so as to set up there a sectarian and undemocratic state, from which one third of the people of Northern Ireland will be excluded. This has not been, at any time over the past few years, a party matter in the House of Commons or in this country at all.

Where the political wildcats of Northern Ireland seek to divide and embitter, all the major parties in Britain have sought to heal and to unite. In the years before 1970, the then Conservative opposition supported the action the Labour government took when we put troops in, in a security role, and issued the Downing Street Declaration about their right to determine their own future.

When Labour was in opposition we supported Mr Heath, Mr Whitelaw and later Mr Francis Pym, first when they suspended the one-sided Stormont parliamentary system which had broken down, then when they devised a new constitution aimed at reconciliation and shared power in Northern Ireland, and again in the initiatives to secure better relations between Ulster and the Irish Republic.

On few constitutional issues in our history have we seen the full government party and the full opposition party voting together for such measures and carrying them with overwhelming majorities.

Agreement was reached by the Northern Ireland Executive in the last few days on arrangements for a new and constructive relationship between North and South. It provides additional reassurance to those in the North who still feared that their way of life would give way to a new all-Ireland system, threatening their religious and political beliefs. There is nothing to fear and they know it.

What has been achieved in Northern Ireland in these last two years provides hope for its future. We are not going to see that set aside by thugs and bullies, behaving as they did in Ballymena last night. We have made it clear as a government—and we speak for the overwhelming majority of the House of

Commons—that we will not negotiate on constitutional or political matters in Northern Ireland with anyone who chooses to operate outside the established political framework; with non-elected self-appointed people who are systematically breaking the law and intimidating the people of Northern Ireland—their fellow citizens and our fellow citizens in the United Kingdom.

We stand by—as our predecessors stood by and still stand by—the decision taken last year that the Northern Ireland assembly and the Northern Ireland Executive provide the only basis for peace, the only basis for order and good government in Northern Ireland.

Today the law is being set aside. British troops are being hampered in the task which was already daunting and unprecedented within a nation supposed to be enjoying the benefits of peace. Those who are now challenging the constitutional authority are denying the fundamental right of every man and woman—the right to work.

They have decided, without having been elected by a single vote, who shall work in Northern Ireland and who shall not. By their action children are prevented from going to school, essential services are in peril.

The payment of social benefits is reduced to chaos through interference with the methods of payment. By their use of force and intimidation they have condemned hundreds of thousands of workers to involuntary unemployment.

What they do not realise—what I hope they do not realise—is how far they may be imperilling the jobs of Northern Ireland for years to come, and this is a province where unemployment is traditionally one of the greatest social evils.

We recognise that behind the situation lie many genuine and deeply held fears. I have to say that these fears are unfounded, that they are being deliberately fostered by people in search of power.

The next few sentences were not what anyone expected.

The people on this side of the water, British parents, have seen their sons vilified and spat upon and murdered. British taxpayers have seen the taxes they have poured out almost without regard to cost—£300 million a year this year with the cost of army operations on top of that—going into Northern Ireland. They see property being destroyed by evil violence and are asked to pick up the bill for rebuilding it. Yet people who benefit from this now viciously defy Westminster, purporting to act as though they were an elected government—people who spend their lives sponging on Westminster and British democracy and then systematically assault democratic methods. Who do these people think they are?

It is when we see the kind of arrogant undemocratic behaviour now going on that the patience of our citizens, parents, taxpayers, becomes strained.

It is no exaggeration to say that with these words the Prime Minister kicked the last props from underneath the Executive. He had delivered two insults to the community as a body: first, he did not make it clear that it was the IRA which was spitting on, vilifying and murdering British troops. He appeared to be lumping the UWC with the IRA.

Secondly, he accused the people the province of being spongers on the central exchequer. It is true that a careful reading of the text suggests that Wilson was referring to the UWC and its supporters, but since by now a very large proportion of Protestants identified with the UWC, the words were interpreted as a general accusation of sponging on Westminster.

The effect was such that some people believed that the words were deliberately inserted in a Machiavellian move to get rid of a troublesome Executive.

The speech was so counter-productive that members of the Executive, in whose support it undoubtedly was given, just groaned and buried their heads in their hands. The wife of Oliver Napier said that if the television set had not been rented she would have thrown something through the screen.

The UWC, watching on a small portable monochrome set, could hardly believe their ears.

'It was a brilliant speech,' Glen Barr roared at the time. 'We couldn't have written better ourselves.'

That speech should have been shown beforehand to people in Northern Ireland who knew the pitfalls, especially to Faulkner and Fitt. The experience of the Northern Ireland Office in directly ruling the province was admittedly pitifully small but not even its head, Merlyn Rees, was allowed input.

The result was an astounding blunder which hastened the destruction of the very ideas it sought to bolster. The following day, people appeared with little bits of sponge pinned to their breasts as a mark of support for the strike.

But the speech was not yet finished. There had been no mention of troops and that is what supporters of the Executive were waiting for. Wilson concluded with the following:

> Tonight I ask for an extension of that patience for as long as it is needed. Tonight I ask for the continued support of a long-suffering people in dealing with a situation in which the law is being set aside and essential services are being interrupted. It is our duty as the United Kingdom parliament and the United Kingdom government to ensure that minorities are protected, not by the condescension of a group of self-appointed persons operating outside the law, but by those who have been elected to ensure that these things shall be done.
>
> The people of Northern Ireland and their democratically elected assembly and Executive have the joint duty of seeing this thing through, on the only basis on which true unity can be achieved: democratic elections, constitutional government and the spirit of tolerance and reconciliation. And in doing that they will have the support of the British government, with our responsibilities within the United Kingdom, and our responsibilities in world affairs, for law and order in Northern Ireland. We intend to see it through with them.

Most of the SDLP agreed that the speech seemed to sign the death warrant of the Executive by uniting the enemies of British policy in Ireland instead of dividing them. Hume, who had been phoned at midnight the previous evening by Faulkner to say in coded fashion that the Cabinet had agreed to the oil plan, had been listening to the speech for only one phrase—something to the effect that the British government would maintain essential services.

The final part of the speech contained those words.

After Wilson, Faulkner's broadcast came next but his speech had the impact of one of Wilson's sponges. In the words of an Alliance member of the Executive, Faulkner was sent into bat but there was no wicket left to defend.

Faulkner's speech included the following words about the loyalists choosing not to play a part in the setting-up of the

Executive. 'Had they come into these discussions in a constructive spirit, it might very well be that we would have a more broadly based Executive and I, for one, would have welcomed this. One cannot however refuse to come in and complain about being shut out at one at the same time.'

Unfortunately for Faulkner it was perfectly possible for that to happen. That was exactly what the loyalists were doing.

FOURTEEN

Sunday morning dawned—and no evidence of the army in filling stations. The SDLP were exasperated beyond measure. Gerry Fitt and Paddy Devlin had both received a phone call on Saturday night asking them to be at Stormont Castle, the Northern Ireland Office, at a quarter to twelve on Sunday morning.

The Northern Ireland Office knew that the SDLP were at the end of their tether and that Paddy Devlin was eager to resign because of inaction by the army.

Rees was caught in a vice. The SDLP was obviously going to do something drastic and bring the Executive down if the troops did not move. But the army had now got the Defence Secretary, Roy Mason, on its side in asserting that taking on the loyalist paramilitaries as well as the IRA was military madness. Rees was trying to head the SDLP off.

Fitt guessed what might be happening and phoned Devlin to meet him half an hour beforehand to plan what they were going to say at Stormont. The growing impossibility of their position was underlined by the fact that to avoid paramilitary barricades, the Deputy Chief Executive and the Minister for Health and Social Services had to scurry through side streets like criminals on the run to achieve their meeting. Fitt was in a very foul mood.

As Fitt was about to get into the car to try to reach his colleague, Devlin phoned to say that he was refusing to go to Stormont. He did not want to hear any more Northern Ireland Office excuses.

So Fitt went to the Northern Ireland Office and found that three of its Westminster politicians were present, Lord Donaldson, spokesman for the Northern Ireland Office in the House of Lords, having joined Rees and Orme. This time Fitt did the talking. He reminded them of the British army mutiny at the Curragh in 1912 over the Ulster question and said that it was not going to happen again. For fifty years, he said, the loyalists had been able to bully their way in everything and that some British government was going to have to confront them. He did not want to see anyone hurt but he thought this was the crunch point. The loyalists must not have victory because there would be repercussions in Irish communities everywhere if they did.

The leaders of the SDLP were to meet at one o'clock, Fitt said. He would announce the cutting of all connections with the Northern Ireland Office because he had bent over backwards to be accommodating and had received nothing in return. And finally an ultimatum. Move the army by eleven o'clock on Monday morning—or else.

The Secretary of State and his lieutenants could be in no doubt that the SDLP had come to the end of the road. In addition, all three Executive party leaders told Rees over an appalling cold lunch exactly what they thought of Wilson's speech. 'Bloody disastrous' was a term frequently used. It was then Rees admitted that he had not known anything about the speech and that the Northern Ireland Office had not been involved in the preparation. He did make the point that the speech was meant for a UK mainland audience but he was now very aware of the extent of political damage wrought by Wilson's words. Oliver Napier thought at the time that events had left Rees pretty shattered. He thought he was an honest decent man left throwing his hands in the air and praying to the Lord.

Prevarication had to end. Rees made immediate arrangements to intrude upon the the Prime Minister's holiday, just begun in the Scilly Isles. They would meet at the naval air station at Culdrose in Cornwall. That afternoon Wilson was compelled to make a final decision on the basis of divided counsel; deep misgivings on the part of his Defence Minister on one hand, the possible collapse of policy in Northern Ireland on the other.

When Fitt returned to his home Paddy Devlin was waiting for him. Devlin was both angry and excited and said he was going to resign that afternoon. The other SDLP members of the administration arrived. Hume drafted a letter for the Northern Ireland Office making no mention of troops but saying that if the British government did not take action to allow the Executive to carry out its responsibilities, all six would resign with effect from six o'clock the next morning, Monday 27 May. All six signed the letter.

Before it was delivered, the opposition leader in Dublin, Jack Lynch, rang Fitt to find out what the SDLP was going to do. As discreetly as he could, Fitt told him that they had decided to send Devlin and Cooper to Dublin to explain. In Northern Ireland people tend to assume that telephones are tapped.

Later that Sunday afternoon, Fitt, Hume and Currie left for Stormont Castle. As Rees had already left for Cornwall to see the Prime Minister, they were received by Orme. Orme read the letter and said he understood the message and called in a secretary to have it typed. He told them that he knew they were not bluffing and Hume surmised from the general tone of his remarks that the Northern Ireland Office at last believed that if oil plan was not implemented, the Executive would fall. This indeed was the message Rees conveyed to Wilson at Culdrose. The Prime Minister then instructed the army to move that night.

Fitt tried to prevent newsmen finding out about the SDLP threat to resign. He thought that when troops eventually did move, it would be seen as having been prompted by Catholic pressure and isolated Catholic communities might suffer as a result. However, Dublin and London newspapers had the report the next morning.

That Sunday, 26 May, the grip of the strike did not seem to become any tighter, perhaps because by that stage every day had become an Ulster sabbath.

Faulkner's Unionist ministers also met. They all believed that the Prime Minister's speech had eroded deeply into their support while making no real progress towards breaking the strike. Some had come to the conclusion that Westminster's policy was to resume direct rule by shooting down the Executive. Their reaction was therefore not all that different from that of the SDLP but it propelled them in a different direction. They were beginning to feel that if the Executive was to be left to conduct the battle with the UWC on its own, then negotiation was fast becoming the only way out in an effort to avoid total defeat.

Negotiation was anathema to the SDLP. John Hume had been on radio that very day calling for Roy Bradford's resignation because he had broken ranks and was calling for negotiation. Other broadcasts that day centred on the Prime Minister's speech. Its tone had put some strain on the bi-partisan approach at Westminster. William Deedes, a Conservative backbencher, former Home Office Minister and frequent commentator on Northern Ireland affairs, felt that Wilson had made a bad mistake in underestimating support for the UWC.

The formal loyalist reply to the speech came from Harry West, leader of the UUUC members at Westminster. The strike was not aimed at a democratic government, West argued. 'The Executive is a group of people appointed by an English politician who is not answerable in any way to the assembly or to the Ulster electorate. It is the appointed Executive which is supposed to represent Northern Ireland in any Council of Ireland. The whole Sunningdale project is thus completely dissociated from any kind of control.'

West moved to the relatively easy 'spongers' target. Calling citizens spongers, he said, was hardly a wise assertion from any quarter, particularly from a prime minister, since no country in the world has its wealth and population evenly distributed.

On behalf of the Ulster people, I repudiate the vile insinuation that we are a community of spongers. We meet the very same taxation demands as every other citizen of the United Kingdom. We are well aware that Exchequer expenditure exceeds the taxation revenue raised here, as indeed it does in Scotland and other parts of the United Kingdom. Are they also spongers?

Wilson's speech allowed the loyalists to cast themselves in the role of protectors of Ulster's good name while associating Faulkner, Fitt and the rest with its detractors. With a friend like the Prime Minister, the Executive hardly needed enemies.

The remaining hope for the Executive lay in successful military action to break the stranglehold of the strikers. Fitt waited in his home, the tension beginning to take its toll. He paced about the house, about the yard and shouted at his family. He listened to the last news broadcast of the day and heard nothing.

A few sleepless hours in bed and then he was wakened by military activity at the army camp opposite his home. He switched on a radio news bulletin at a quarter to six and still heard nothing of interest. His resignation and that of his colleagues took effect in a few minutes. Desperately he rang the Northern Ireland Office and asked a civil servant for news.

'Not just yet,' came the reply, 'but in a few minutes.'

'I hope this is not a disaster,' Fitt said to his wife.

****

In point of fact, the army had begun implementing the oil plan at five o'clock that Monday morning, 27 May. There was no opposition as they entered the refinery at Sydenham in Belfast, the oil storage installation on the Pennyburn Road in Londonderry and the twenty-one filling stations dotted about the province.

Seven filling stations were in Belfast, two in Londonderry, and one each in Larne, Ballymena, Portadown, Lisburn, Bangor, Omagh, Enniskillen, Newry, Armagh, Dungannon, Coleraine and Downpatrick.

The first effect seemed a propaganda victory for the UWC who were supplying petrol to over 140 stations and bulk users. These supplies were abruptly terminated. To the man in the street it seemed a poor exchange. Ninety minutes later, as envisaged in the plan, the workers in Belfast's domestic gas plant alongside the refinery walked out. The gas undertaking issued urgent bulletins to mains gas users in Belfast and the surrounding towns of Bangor, Newtownards, Carrickfergus, Holywood and Lisburn telling them to turn off gas appliances immediately and leave them off for fear of explosions.

During the rest of the morning the grain mills in Belfast which supplied the bakeries with flour and the farmers with animal feed came to a halt. Barricades reappeared on roads throughout the province. The main road between Belfast and Dublin was blocked in several places, as Devlin and Cooper found when they tried to return after meeting the Irish Cabinet in Dublin. This pleased the loyalists and many other Unionists. Frequent visits to Dublin by SDLP Executive members during the past five months of shared government had angered Protestants, who believed that through such visits the Irish government was exerting undue influence on the Northern Ireland administration.

Alison Lennox, manager of the Belfast oil refinery, had received a long-awaited telephone call at ten past five in the morning to say that the Department of Commerce was taking over his plant. It needed skilled technicians round the clock and he could not guarantee they would remain at their posts, so Lennox ordered a six-hour shut-down procedure. He was relieved that he managed it because there was also a 'panic' button which sets in train a crash shutdown, spectacular because all the gas in the system is flamed off. If that occurred restarting was a greater problem. There were panic buttons all over the plant and this led to problems.

Soldiers thought the tanker loading area of the refinery had been sabotaged. They could get nothing to work. However, this was not the case. The workers had cleared out in a hurry and had shut down the pumping system by pressing the emergency stop buttons. When this happened, they 'tripped out' the whole of the pump switching system back to a sub-station.

Army engineers eventually worked out what had happened, and by three o'clock that afternoon the loading of tankers was in progress. Lennox was not too happy with the careless way soldiers handled highly inflammable spirit. They spilt a lot of volatile fuels and did not always earth the vehicles to guard against a spark from static electricity. One such spark could have put a big hole in the oil plan.

Another problem soon became public. The soldiers were not always sure what product they were dealing with. An oil refinery produces various grades of oil, from thick black oil for burning in power stations to light distillates such as petrol and paraffin. Oil is labelled in seconds; very heavy oil for burning is 6,500 second, a small factory boiler might use 220 second oil and diesel oil used by road vehicles and central heating is 35 second. But the Belfast oil refinery was using another set of number labels unrelated to the rating in seconds of the oil. So when an engineer from a hospital rang up and asked for 35 second oil, the civil servant in the refinery looked up the list of products, saw one called F35 and sent it on its way. The F35 oil was thick black fuel normally burnt in marine boilers. Luckily the soldier on the delivery used his head, more particularly his nose, and realised in time that whatever he had brought, it was not 35 second diesel oil. Other customers were not so lucky. Paraffin was delivered to petrol stations and ended up in some cars.

These mistakes were not made by the army but by the hard-pressed civil servants thrown into a crisis situation with minimal training, if any. The remarkable aspect of the operation was not that mistakes were made, but that so few were made during the deliveries of the 1,800 tons of product made in the last four days of the strike.

The oil plan never moved as much oil as the unofficial UWC plan. Even the problem of serving Derry's gas works had been solved. The oil shop stewards had persuaded the co-ordinating committee that naphtha had to be delivered to the city and on Sunday night two tankers had been loaded for driving to Derry the following morning. The army operation intervened before they set off.

The tankers would only have been temporary relief for the city. If the stoppage had continued for very much larger into a third week, the UWC and the UDA would have gone for 'sudden death', as they called it. No electricity and no oil products. As it happened, the UWC did not immediately close all its filling stations because the UDA needed fuel and they were not going to get it from government stations. However, secret plans were in place to close the UWC stations quite soon (they were not being supplied from the occupied refinery anyway). But in the meantime, full petrol tankers were to be hidden and used as filling points in the last resort for UDA vehicles only. This would have been the final application of the oil weapon.

The final criticism made of the oil plan was the manner of its implementation. The installations were being requisitioned by the Department of Commerce, not the army, yet it was the army who rolled up at five o'clock in the morning. The civil servants came three hours later waving bits of paper. If the procedure had been the other way round, there was a chance that civilian workers might have thought a little longer before disappearing. There were political gains to be had by demonstrating that it was a civilian takeover.

For a brief moment the Executive looked a little stronger now that the army had moved very clearly in its support but very soon its edifice began to crumble and the end came very fast. Gerry Fitt had been right to try to suppress the news of the SDLP threat to resign. The twenty-one government petrol stations had been bequeathed from earlier emergency plans which assumed an IRA threat. Many of the chosen stations were therefore in the middle of staunchly loyalist areas and had to be protected like mini-forts. The soldiers were taunted with names like 'Corporal Fitt's army'.

More seriously there was an immediate crisis in electricity, again anticipated by government. The UWC said that preparations to close the complete electricity system were under way but that workers would remain in Ballylumford power station for reasons of safety. This masked the real drama.

Ballylumford was running three 120 megawatt sets, a total of 360 megawatts therefore available. The UWC now demanded that one set be taken off. The NIES replied that the system would be unsafe if a further 120 megawatts were subtracted and refused. The management said that if the workers walked out, they would shut down the whole system.

This information was passed to Hume as the minister responsible. He was still trying to have his electricity plan put into effect, which would provide power for the already split grid in the less Protestant north and west from the Coolkeeragh station. For Hume, there were positive advantages if the UWC abandoned Ballylumford. He could concentrate on serving the other half of the grid, leaving the Protestant heartland to take the brunt of the UWC closedown of electricity. The major portion of the Protestant population of Northern Ireland lived in Belfast and towns within thirty to forty miles of the city.

The NIES management was having difficulty because the technical knowledge of shop floor workers was insufficient to appreciate what could happen to the system in certain circumstances. The problem was the fault levels, the reason why the grid had been split almost a week before on Tuesday 21 May. In greater detail, to protect generators, transformers, transmission lines and the public, every electricity system must have automatic sensing devices which will detect a fault and switch off part of the system. A typical fault might be the breakage of a power line. The fault-sensing devices must be able to pick up that event and switch off the power before anyone could touch a live cable. Normally the switch-off is virtually instantaneous.

The problem was that the sensing devices depended on a certain minimum level of current flowing through the lines and areas of the grid would have been without that protection if one of the three remaining generating sets was taken off. The NIES would prefer to close down the complete system. The problem was complex, too complex to explain to impatient workers and so complex that afterwards, computer studies were made for a more complete evaluation.

During the strike the workers tended to accept the technical advice provided by the NIES management at face value—if not at once, then after a little talking. This was possible as long as the NIES did not attempt to put Hume's plan into effect by running up Coolkeeragh to full power using only Catholic workers. At the time, Coolkeeragh was supplying a tiny 60 megawatts from a turbine normally used for topping up at times of extra peak load.

But once troops had been deployed in the oil industry the mood of the UWC changed. They did not accept what the NIES was saying about fault levels and demanded a reduction of power by one third by taking off one 120 megawatt set at Ballylumford. The workers walked out, leaving an ultimatum. Take one set off by midnight or else. The technical staff remained on site, but it should be remembered that most lived in Larne, just across the closed harbour. Larne was tightly in the grip of the UDA and the police or army could not protect the technicians or their families if they had attempted to keep the station running by themselves.

In desperation the NIES technical director, Jim Smith, gathered a group of engineers and technicians and left headquarters in Belfast for Ballylumford. When they arrived, there were no workers and the station was completely in the hands of technical staff. They held a meeting and reviewed their options, which were: doing as the UWC demanded and running the system at fault levels utterly unacceptable in normal conditions or shutting down all three remaining sets. In effect closing down the main part of the system. Closing down one set at Ballylumford would mean running the system outside their terms of reference. If anything went wrong, if millions of pounds worth of damage was sustained by the plant, if somebody was killed because the safety devices could not work, a panel of inquiry might very well question their actions.

But top engineers like Jim Smith knew the rule book had no rules for a situation like this. It had never been envisaged, so in the end they decided to do as the UWC demanded, shut down one set and run the risks. They were aware of the political significance of shutting down completely and considered that their over-riding duty was to maintain some electricity as long as possible. They remained adamant that they could not put Hume's plan into effect on the grounds that it was sectarian.

This angered Hume very much. He had found it incredible that the army could not run the power stations, but like the workers, he himself may not have realised the complicated nature, not so much of running a power station, but of managing the power once it was within the supply grid. As it was, the NIES warned Hume that the system with only two sets running at Ballylumford would be so far out of balance that a single fault could trigger a complete blackout. It is reasonable to assume that army technicians would have had no experience of dealing with the Northern Ireland grid. But what about the naval technicians who had been flown in and were ready to step in? Hume wondered why they had arrived from various quarters of the globe if they too could not handle the grid. Information reaching Hume throughout the strike indicated that a substantial number of senior and middle management of the NIES had been ready to remain at their posts in distribution if service personnel helped maintain generation. However, when the time arrived for such action the NIES people refused. Hume was convinced that somehow they had been pressurised into changing their minds and his finger pointed at top managers within the NIES. Hume believed they were being sectarian; they believed he was being sectarian. Neither accusation was valid. Neither fully understood the imperatives of the other.

Twenty-fours hours. That was how long the technicians said they could run Ballylumford for. In every sense the Executive had twenty-four hours of shaky power left.

The SDLP assembly party met and endorsed the action of its leaders over the weekend and the threat to the unity of the Executive from that quarter had passed. Now Faulkner's party began to show real signs of trouble. First Nelson Elder, a backbencher, said he could no longer support the Executive after the use of troops. Many of his colleagues agreed with him. That evening, the chairman of Faulkner's backbenchers said that talks with the UWC would have to take place some time. Even the Alliance Party leader, Napier, found it necessary to reiterate that the Executive was ready to talk to elected representatives, in other words, the UUUC politicians.

The Executive and Northern Ireland Office looked for signs of shaken UWC resolve now that the army had been used for strike-breaking action—and found none. Far from it. All three loyalist political leaders issued statements to the effect that they wanted direct rule from Westminster and would eat grass to achieve it. The UWC had imposed even more drastic sanctions and there seemed to be little reaction from the public against the men at Hawthornden Road for doing so. The UWC had even said that the burying of the dead was to stop and henceforth this was to be the responsibility of the army. Now that the army had begun to assume responsibility for some services, the strategy was to heap as much work on the troops (now 17,500) as possible. There was no mood of despondency in the warren of little streets of Protestant Belfast. After a loyalist rally in Sandy Row, people danced in the streets. They smelt victory.

And by lunchtime that Monday Faulkner was smelling defeat. The gamble of using the army had failed; the people who began telling him so were his own civil service heads. By himself, Faulkner met the departmental permanent secretaries and the picture they painted was frightening. The top civil servants knew that the NIES could not carry on, that animal feed firms and bakeries were halting, that water and sewage were going to be immediate problems (parts of Derry would be without water that night) and if there was violence, the movement of oil by the army could become impossible.

They told him the Northern Ireland farms would not have any breeding stock left by the end of the week, that the first deaths of people because of the collapse of essential services would be among the very young, the very old and the very weak—and they would begin within thirty-six hours.

The final blow was an indication from these men that the civil service might consider its own situation impossible. When this happened to an organisation within which loyalty to government is almost ingested with mother's milk, Faulkner was finally convinced that there was little support left for him in the country. He had earlier begun to think in terms of a mediator, perhaps Sir Fred Catherwood, the Ulster-born industrialist and advisor to the Westminster government, or Lord Grey, the former governor of Northern Ireland.

On the following morning, Tuesday 28 May, Faulkner's twelve backbenchers met and made it clear they would call publicly for mediation or a line of communication with the UWC.

An Executive meeting, the last, began at eleven o'clock in the morning. The final collapse came quickly. The Unionists said that there would have to be talks and were supported by the Alliance members. The three members from the SDLP present, Devlin still being in Dublin with Cooper, voted against. There was therefore a majority vote for opening talks and armed with this Faulkner walked from Parliament Buildings to Stormont Castle to ask Rees for talks or mediation.

As he did so, he saw a demonstration of farmers gathering on the long sweeping drive leading up through the parkland to the imposing front of Stormont, tractors and farm machinery as far as his eye could see, their placards demanding negotiations, resignations, and 'no' to everything the Executive stood for.

When Rees heard what Faulkner had to say, he replied the way Faulkner expected. The British government would not talk under duress. Faulkner then handed in the resignations of all Unionist members of the Executive.

Wearily he returned past the demonstrators to the Executive meeting where he informed its members that the resignations of the Unionists had been accepted. Once again came the expressions of regard for Faulkner as leader but the emotion this time was adulterated by the memory of the time only six days before when they thought the phasing agreement would end the Executive. Now the phasing was of no consequence, nor was the Council of Ireland, or the legal framework or anything else to do with the brave experiment of the Sunningdale communique. It had all collapsed. British policy in Ireland was in tatters.

The Alliance Party thought Faulkner's resignation had been a terrible mistake. It believed that both sides were indulging in brinkmanship and if the Executive had been able to hold on another seventy-two hours, support for the UWC would have crumbled instead. Some members of the UWC even thought the same privately. But none of that mattered now either.

The UWC and Harry Murray had won. The loyalist paramilitaries had won, particularly Andy Tyrie and the UDA. The loyalist politicians had won. The next day the strike was called off, the delay caused by the paramilitaries wanting to hold out until a promise of fresh elections was secured.

But on Wednesday 29 May the population voted with its feet and went back to work. The fall of the Executive brought with it the fall of the monolithic support the UWC had managed to attract.

In the Executive meeting room many were openly in tears as Brian Faulkner spoke the epitaph of his extraordinary Northern Ireland government.

'After five months of being able to work together, Catholic and Protestant, I hope that one thing can remain—that we do not attack each other on a sectarian basis ever again.'

CONCLUSION

The greatest single cause of the success of the stoppage was the deep sense of political grievance felt by the majority Protestant community.

It began as William Whitelaw was fashioning his new constitution for Northern Ireland during the latter part of 1973. The loyalists were correct when they argued that the elections for the assembly that year were ambiguous. It was never clear whether a vote for Faulkner's Unionists was a vote for power sharing with the SDLP. What Faulkner stood for only became clear after the elections, when he negotiated at the Sunningdale Civil Service College at the end of 1973, believing he had secured viable terms for power sharing.

It was always going to be difficult to overcome a gut reaction among Protestants that to admit Catholics into a Northern Ireland government would be a betrayal of their principles, of the principles of Unionism. Their political history during the twentieth century could almost be confined to their fighting the rest of Ireland, which was republican Catholic. Nonetheless, power sharing was a difficult target for the Protestants, who were learning that to resist from a narrow anti-Catholic standpoint was regarded elsewhere, particularly in Great Britain, as uncivilised and unacceptable. Within their own ranks there was a considerable number of Protestants who felt that naked anti-Catholicism was morally wrong, certainly pragmatically wrong. Therefore the loyalists always said they were against enforced power sharing. It is also worth remembering that loyalist politicians like William Craig and Glen Barr, the strike leader, afterwards declared themselves in favour of voluntary power sharing of some kind with the SDLP.

There were no qualms about opposing the Council of Ireland proposal outright. Opposition to this could be expressed in pure political terms. In a situation where the constitution of the Republic of Ireland explicitly claimed jurisdiction of the six counties of Northern Ireland, the Council could easily be represented as retreat before that claim. And of course, in Protestant and Unionist eyes, if the SDLP wanted a Council of Ireland, then it simply *must* be a step towards Irish unity.

The setting-up of a subsidiary government excluding the loyalists was always a doubtful gamble. When the loyalists were reminded that they had excluded themselves, they retorted that they had been excluded by the terms of reference at the outset of the Sunningdale talks. For the gamble to win, the British government needed a period of successful administration with as little controversy as possible. Such a beginning would have created opportunities for the new institution to generate momentum and stability. It was never allowed this stability; the core institution, which was the assembly, was crippled by loyalist boycott.

Though it was never put formally in these terms, the meaningful participation of Catholics in the government of Northern Ireland was expected to undermine support for Sinn Féin and the IRA, leading to a reduction if not an end of violence. But the IRA continued to fight for the destruction of the political entity of Northern Ireland and disregarded the reforms which put Catholics and nationalists in controlling positions. So the Protestants felt that they had yielded much and received nothing in return. Thus the strike was to win back what had been lost, which was Protestant control.

Another major blow to the short-lived Executive was the general election of 28 February 1974. This was caused by the miners' strike in Great Britain and fought on UK economic issues, but in Northern Ireland it became a referendum on the Sunningdale agreement. Eleven of the twelve Northern Ireland members of Parliament were against Sunningdale (Gerry Fitt's was the lone Ulster vote for it). From that time on there was an unending string of rumours about possible defections from Faulkner to the loyalists, and perceptibly increasing hostility among the Faulknerites to the Council of Ireland, which they had previously accepted.

As a consequence, the ratification of the Sunningdale agreement was delayed and remained a central issue of Northern Ireland politics. Part of the blame is to be laid at the door of the Executive itself for taking so long to arrive at a phasing arrangement which would get the Faulknerites off the hook, and part at the door of the British and Irish governments for taking so long to agree the details of law enforcement procedures on both sides of the border (also part of the Sunningdale agreement).

There is a case to be made that the Executive was created prematurely. Those issues should have been settled first in order to give the new Stormont government a less perilous political foundation.

Nevertheless at the beginning the loyalist politicians were very loath to give their support to the UWC strike. The same was true of the general Protestant population at large. On the first day of the stoppage only an estimated ten per cent of the workforce stayed away from work. Everyone had in mind the loyalist strike of the year before which had been discredited by the violent actions of loyalist paramilitaries.

The Executive and the Northern Ireland Office also saw the advent of the UWC strike in terms of the previous strike but failed to see the major difference developing. While there was initial widespread intimidation, there was no overt violence, or at least, nothing like the scale of the 1973 strike. The UDA and other paramilitaries avoided the extent of violence which had so alienated respectable Protestants. They played cat and mouse.

The army saw what was happening but interpreted it wrongly. The army thought it demonstrated a federated paramilitary organisation, far far larger than the IRA, preparing for a shooting war. The army could not have been more wrong. The UDA orders were to fall back and to melt away if confronted by determined action by the army and police. It meant that the new and inexperienced Secretary of State was given wrong advice by the army and the Executive was unable to counter it. Rees trusted the army.

In those first three critical days of the stoppage the army should have mobilised every available man and cleared the roads of barricades in Belfast and Larne. The strike had very little support or organisation behind it and the Ulster Workers' Council was a front for the paramilitaries. Therefore the UDA and the rest of the paramilitaries were forced to embark on a massive campaign of intimidation to start the ball rolling. The resentment engendered by this tactic is evidenced in the volume of complaints pouring into police phones, to the army and journalists. The call for strong action from the many victims was loud, clear and insistent.

Having established that, the use of the army to clear the roads could only have had two outcomes. If the paramilitary organisations continued to fall back, the roads would have been clear, certainly clear enough long enough to allow people to work.

If the paramilitaries abandoned their restraint, or fell into the trap of rioting or shooting, then what happened in 1973 would probably have happened again. The support of middle Protestants would never have accumulated and the strike would have petered out. The unified Protestant support would never have coalesced and the loyalist politicians might very well have ended up dissociating themselves. All the army had to be careful about in those circumstances was not to over-react and give the loyalists their own 'Bloody Sunday' mini-massacre.

Some of the leaders of the UWC and of the UDA, including Tyrie himself, agreed that if the army had moved decisively at the beginning, their stoppage would have been in severe difficulties.

If political acumen was not one of the army's strong points, this is understandable, but the same can hardly said of the Northern Ireland Office which had the political responsibility of directing the army and police. An early army operation to clear the barricades would not have needed frantic dashes to Cornwall to put into effect. The police were a relatively small force of approximately 4,300 at that time with only 1,500 available for Belfast. By contrast, the army had up to 17,500 men and was the only force with a realistic capability of tackling barricades, of which there were over 800.

This battle was too important to leave to the soldiers, but that is what Rees and Orme did. Though he was not Secretary of State during the 1973 strike, Merlyn Rees ought to have done his homework, or at least listened to people who had lived through the experience, people like Brian Faulkner, Gerry Fitt and the other Executive members. But Rees preferred to listen to his generals telling him about wars on two fronts and by the time he had finished rubbing his brow, the second front actually existed.

Those who were against the strike (a large number) plus those who were wavering (another large number) looked on with incredulity as the authorities adopted a wait-and-see posture on the manicured slopes of Stormont. Control of the roads was allowed to pass to the loyalist paramilitaries with little more than a skirmish. The inaction of constituted authority cut the feet from under the power-sharing Executive more cruelly than any election result, than any tirade from loyalists or any outrage from the IRA.

When government was seen not to govern, it could be argued that the loyalist politicians of the UUUC were left with no alternative but to support the stoppage. At first they were not happy with the use of the strike weapon and a couple of UUUC assembly members publicly criticised what was happening in the early days. Support from them for the UWC and the paramilitaries was not inevitable. Indeed the co-ordinating committee resented the late arrival of the politicians on the bandwagon. All this was known and ignored as weaponry in the government armoury.

But the Executive was also guilty of fiddling while its Rome burnt. For the first eight critical days its members were embroiled in two major squabbles which prompted one resignation and made others a possibility. The row over phasing the Council of Ireland came within seconds of demolishing the Executive. Rees and the Cabinet in London were partly to blame for forcing the pace. It should have been recognised that if the Executive did not win against the UWC, no other issue mattered. A moratorium should have been declared on all secondary issues while the decks were cleared for the crucial battle.

The failure of the trade union marches back to work was inevitable and predicted by very many people, supporters and non-supporters alike. Their failure starkly exposed just how much ground the government had lost in that first week. The operation to clear the roads for them was useless.

By the second Friday of the strike, the authorities had shown themselves unable or unwilling to control electricity, the running of factories, flour and animal feed mills, the supply of oil and petrol, free movement on the roads. The strike co-ordinating committee at Hawthornden Road was demonstrating the action and the exercise of power in the same measure as the authorities exhibited bad judgement, inaction and vacillation.

Those who lent their support to the Northern Ireland Labour Party and New Ulster Movement group in an effort to initiate dialogue were people of substance, whose 'moderate' credentials would be difficult to call into question. Their natural tendency was to support lawfully constituted authority and yet it was these very people who, by the end of the first week, were appalled by government ineptitude and did everything in their power to reach Rees to advise a change of course.

The government was right not to enter negotiations on constitutional matters with the UWC. The UWC was a small organisation which, at the most, held sway in the workforce of power stations and which had become the creature of the paramilitaries. It was scarcely heard of before the strike which bore its name and what there was of it disappeared afterwards. Of course the government could have talked to the UUUC politicians who had a valid mandate, but the strike had happened because there had been insufficient common ground for negotiation during the preceding six months.

However, the basic difficulty for the Northern Ireland Office was that entering negotiations with anyone would have meant sufficient resignations from the Executive to engender its collapse. In a sense, all the players were trapped in the drama until something snapped and that is bad politics.

The bad politics of the Northern Ireland Office were compounded by allowing the military tail to wag the dog. Having said that, towards the end of the strike the very evident reluctance of the army to enter the arena of strike breaking, as distinct from keeping order and peace, was well founded. The army could never have handled the provision of every essential service, and any attempt to do so was bound to fail and perhaps lead to armed confrontation with Protestant paramilitaries. Above all, the army could not keep electricity flowing, which was the major key to keeping factories turning. It was doubtful if the better qualified navy personnel could have done so either without the co-operation of the NIES control engineers. Civilian engineers from other parts of the United Kingdom did not materialise.

On the last Friday night a section of Protestant paramilitaries went on the rampage in Co. Antrim, murdering two innocent Catholics and committing other outrages. This did not provoke prolonged revulsion against the strike within its core support. It certainly would have done so in the early stages of the strike, but by that Friday the mood, the conditions, the expectations had all changed. The army noted this and knew that if it ended up exchanging fire with loyalist gunmen, the mass of the Protestant population would most likely be hostile to established authority, something which had never happened yet. At worst it would have meant that the United Kingdom government was in conflict in a three-cornered fight with the whole of the population of Northern Ireland and its position would have been untenable.

In effect though, this fact sets the limit on loyalist opposition to central government so long as Unionists see maintenance of the union with Great Britain as their bedrock political aim. If the day ever came when an exasperated Britain told the loyalists that their loyalism was anti-British (which is what Wilson was telling them in his speech) to the point where Westminster no longer wished to maintain the union, then Unionism is in huge trouble. A union is a bridge. It can be severed at either end.

The strike provided food for thought in one or two narrowly defined areas. One is broadcasting.

When the lack of electricity turned off television sets, the small battery-powered radio became important. Therefore BBC Northern Ireland, which had a near monopoly of sound broadcasting, became very important. (RTE radio from Dublin was also heard but had nothing like the penetration of BBC.) Broadcasters had been very aware of the sensitivities of the audience since the divisions in society and civil strife erupted once again in 1968. Newsmen were broadcasting to a society divided within itself and, unlike committed Northern Ireland newspapers, their news permeated the homes of Catholic and Protestants alike. During the strike, all newsmen became hypersensitive, and broadcasters more so because politicians dabbled in, interfered with and sought to influence broadcasting in a manner not known in newspapers for centuries.

BBC Northern Ireland had a truncated regional radio service consisting of local programming inserted into the Radio Four wavelength. This was expanded during the emergency to allow news bulletins roughly every hour. There were problems, first with the UWC and the loyalist paramilitaries, then with the Executive and the Northern Ireland Office, and finally with the IRA. Quite a list to have come up against in a mere two weeks.

The strike co-ordinating committee was very unhappy with the comprehensive reports of the intimidation of the first few days of the strike, so much so that it considered whether it might be feasible to take over the BBC studios. They also considered the possiblity of blowing up the BBC's main radio transmitter masts for the purpose of supplanting BBC broadcasts with their own pirate service on the same wavelength.

Then the authorities became annoyed at the reports of road blockages and barricades which they thought played into the hands of the UWC by giving the impression that every road in the province was blocked. It is hard to see what else the BBC could do. The government was inclined to forget that there were people who really needed to know where barricades were, such as those who were trying to get to work, and Catholics. A list of the roads still open might have given an even worse impression.

Later, much of the criticism from government distilled into a distinct yet vague feeling that the BBC was somehow pro-UWC. This probably arose from the fact that as the UWC grew stronger, the BBC reflected this. In the end the BBC, along with every other news organisation, was forced to pay heed to statements by the UWC because the latter was controlling so much. When the UWC said that deliveries of animal feed would halt, they halted. When it announced that Belfast was to be left without domestic gas, it happened. When it threatened to remove all remaining workers from the power stations if the army was used, it did so. All of this was reported. In the end, Harry Murray and his colleagues shelved plans to move against the BBC because the co-ordinating committee was pleased at the coverage, but anger or pleasure from that quarter played no part in the BBC's editorial decisions.

By contrast, the material coming from Stormont was weak, reflecting as it did a supine response to the challenge. The SDLP felt very strongly that the BBC had been biased towards the loyalists. (This was an extraordinary change round. For years the loyalists were convinced that the BBC was against them. Camera crews and journalists were repeatedly attacked at loyalist rallies and the BBC newsroom was petrol bombed by loyalists while I myself was in it.) Towards the end Merlyn Rees openly acknowledged to Sandy Scott in London that government reaction had been a public relations disaster. In those circumstances there was little any news outlet could do, but that did not stop the BBC being blamed.

To cap it all, shortly after the strike ended an IRA car bomb exploded outside the front door of the BBC, wrecking practically every room at the front of the seven storey-building, mercifully hurting no one. As one BBC man said wearily picking his way through the shambles, 'Message received and understood.'

It is interesting that the same pressures were not being applied to Ulster Television, the commercial television broadcaster in the province, even though much the same material was being broadcast from its Ormeau Road studios, partly because radio rather than television became the most important broadcast medium when power for television sets was not available.

The UWC strike demonstrated to the Protestants of the North that they had a weapon short of civil war and it could be used to thwart the will of the United Kingdom government and, if need be, the will of the Republic of Ireland. They could make the place ungovernable under certain specific conditions.

The first condition was having somebody other than themselves who cared that the place was being reduced to a shambles. The United Kingdom government of Harold Wilson cared only because the Executive was in place. Even so, there were quite a number of influential people in Whitehall who held views similar to those of Kevin MacNamara, who said he would rather see the sewage rise in the streets than negotiate. Another administration might have folded its arms and watched the Protestant population inflict whatever damage upon themselves they wished. After all, that is what happened when the Republicans tried a hunger strike in the eighties. The hunger strikers were allowed to die.

The second condition was solid support among the Protestant population. The UWC strike achieved that because of skilful application of intimidation, because there was a definable target to aim at and because there was pusillanimous reaction from the authorities which in turn funnelled and generated more support towards the strike. The loyalists under the Rev. Ian Paisley tried the strike weapon again in 1977 and its limitations immediately became apparent. First, there was no monolithic body of support. The UDA was in support, the UVF against. Paisley's fellow loyalist leaders, Craig and West, were opposed to it. In Stormont Castle as Secretary of State was Roy Mason, who had been Defence Minister at the time of the UWC strike. He was a decisive and often aggressive man who made sure he did not back into the same cul-de-sac as Merlyn Rees. Resolute action by the army and the police kept commuter routes open right from the beginning. And of course, there was no soft target like power sharing and a prospective Council of Ireland. The lessons of 1974 had been learnt in one quarter and forgotten in another, so the 1977 strike petered out, much to the embarrassment of Paisley.

In the time since May 1974, Westminster has tried a constitutional convention, another assembly, formal and informal inter-party talks, everything imaginable to try to re-establish a power-sharing subsidiary government—and for at almost twenty years it has failed. To that extent the perpetrators of the UWC strike achieved their aims. But in that time the death toll has risen from just over a thousand to well over 3,000, added to which are tens of thousands of injuries and millions upon millions of pounds' damage. In that time, as with the trench warfare of the First World War, the battle lines have shifted little over the years.

The main points for an interim peace are substantially within the document put forward by the dying Northern Ireland Labour Party to the Northern Ireland Office on Sunday 19 May 1974. It took only a mere four years of killing in the First World War for the participants to recognise they had fought themselves to a standstill and to negotiate. The struggle in Northern Ireland looks as though it will last my working life and into that of my children.

Predictions are a hazard at the best of times, but I am beginning to believe that the loyalist cause will be defeated if it cannot identify an achievable strategic aim and advance towards it. Standing still while everybody else moves is not an option. The Council of Ireland, which the loyalists hated more than internal power sharing, has been effectually established over their heads under another name—the Anglo-Irish Agreement—by soverign governments in Dublin and London. Through it and parallel with it the Republic of Ireland has formal and informal influence in the running of Northern Ireland. It might be said, and even been perceived in some Protestant quarters, that the workings of the Anglo-Irish Agreement have not been to the detriment of any core activity or belief held dear by the loyalists—except of course the principle of its existing at all. Protests against the new Agreement have ceased except for a few faded signs.

To achieve stability, the question of sovereignty must be addressed by loyalist political thinkers. This is where it becomes necessary to identify with great accuracy the purpose of loyalism, or Unionism or whatever the Ulster Protestants wish to call their political position. If the ultimate aim of Unionism remains the protection of the Protestant way of life, then detaching the question of British sovereignty might ultimately be the best way of achieving it. Parliament and government at Westminster have an imperfect understanding of political Protestantism and even less sympathy. In other words, the union with Great Britain may not be the best way to secure a Protestant way of life.

The Union flag has been made the emblem of Protestantism in Northern Ireland but in the rest of the United Kingdom, particularly in England, it stands for values at best indifferent, at worst both repugnant and hostile to the conservative strain of Protestantism found in Ulster. The union with Great Britain may ultimately snap under such a strain, of which the UWC strike was an ominous symptom.

A breakup of the union is being assisted by an ever-increasing number of Catholics within Northern Ireland's border, by a decline in the importance of national sovereignty within a uniting European Community and by continued and perhaps rising discomfort in Washington with a perceived British support for a discredited Protestant separatism.

A succession of British governments have been adamant that there will no re-establishment of a parliament and subordinate administration in Belfast which returns Northern Ireland to undiluted Protestant government. In London's view, the Unionists were allowed a relatively free hand in the half century up to March 1972 (when the old Stormont parliament in Belfast was finally prorogued amid chaos on the streets) to make partition work. However, the Unionists failed to appreciate that their prime task in the interests of the survival of their subsidiary government was to create Catholic Unionists. Instead they followed policies diametrically opposed to this concept, making Catholics most unwelcome as Unionist Party members. Thus they shut Catholics out of the political process and denied them any stake in Stormont and its attendant institutions. Warning rumblings expressed as repeated outbreaks of rioting and small bombing campaigns throughout those fifty years were not perceived as portents of anything serious, still less the eventual creation of the Provisional IRA and Northern Ireland as a battlefield.

It was not totally the fault of the Unionists. It is too easy to forget that they were operating in a context of smouldering hostility between Dublin and London in the wake of a bloody and vicious war of Irish independence which had resulted in an imposed partition of the island, never accepted by Irish nationalists on either side of the border. At the time of the Second World War, feelings were still so raw that Dublin refused to join the United Kingdom against Nazi Germany. So when the Unionists at Stormont were denying Catholics and nationalists a place at the fireside in Northern Ireland, the British government was disinclined to intervene and broadly left Stormont to its own Irish stew. The stew eventually boiled over and cannot now be put back into the original pot.

The context then changed dramatically. The Irish war of independence slipped further into history, so did the Second World War, so did strident nationalism in a maturing self-confident Irish republic. At last London and Dublin began serious talking about the partition of Ireland and what to do with the Protestants and Unionists.

Some Unionists, but not all or even most, as the UWC strike vividly demonstrated, realised that their future was now on the agenda of tentative moves towards a final settlement between Ireland and the United Kingdom; that if Northern Ireland was to survive much longer as a separate political entity within the United Kingdom, then accommodation had to be reached with the Northern Ireland Catholics and nationalists. In a hostile world and among the quirks that constitute history, Irish nationalists may have ended up the only friends available to Unionists. That essentially was what the Sunningdale agreement and the power-sharing Executive was about. If this view proves in time to be correct, then the UWC strike was no victory for the loyalists or Unionists. It was the beginning of the end of their brand of Unionism.

Paradoxically the place to find sympathy for the concept of a Protestant state for a Protestant people is among those who have a Catholic state for a Catholic people. I refer to Dublin and the Irish republic. The two conditions either side of the Irish border are historically reverse images of each other and reactions to each other. The Irish government may be the one authority that would be politically capable of giving Protestants much of what they want with at least the acquiescence, more likely the relief and active support, of American and European opinion. The difference between the Irish republic and everywhere else in the world for Ulster Protestants is that the Irish Republic actively wants them within agreed terms. Unfortunately, it remains a heresy to articulate within Unionism that the protection the vulnerable Northern Protestants seek and the peace they desperately need could be negotiated from under the Irish tricolour and not the Union flag.

It has been forgotten that Protestant orange was deliberately incorporated as one the colours of the Irish tricolour. It never was part of flag of the United Kingdom and never ever will be.

APPENDIX A

THE SUNNINGDALE AGREEMENT

The following is the agreed communique of December 1973 issued after the talks which finalised the establishment of the power-sharing coalition government of Northern Ireland under the Chief Executive, Brian Faulkner. It became informally known as the Sunningdale Agreement.

1. The conference between the British and Irish Governments and the parties involved in the Northern Ireland Executive (designate) met at Sunningdale on 6, 7, 8 and 9 December 1973.

2. During the conference, each delegate stated their position on the status of Northern Ireland.

3. The Taoiseach said that the basic principle of the conference was that the participants had tried to see what measure of benefit to all the people concerned could be secured. In doing so, all had reached accommodation with one another on practical arrangements. But none had compromised, and none had asked others to compromise, in relation to basic aspirations. The people of the Republic, together with a minority in Northern Ireland as represented by the SDLP delegation, continued to uphold the aspiration towards a united Ireland. The only unity they wanted to see was a unity established by consent.

4. Mr Brian Faulkner said that the delegates from Northern Ireland came to the conference as representatives of apparently incompatible sets of political aspirations who had found it possible to reach agreement to join together in government because each accepted that in doing so they were

not sacrificing principles or aspirations. The desire of the majority to remain part of the United Kingdom, as represented by the Unionist and Alliance delegations, remained firm.

5. The Irish Government fully accepted and solemnly declared that there could be no change in the status of Northern Ireland until a majority of the people of Northern Ireland desired a change in status.

The British Government solemnly declared that it was, and would remain, their policy to support the wishes of the majority of people in Northern Ireland. The present status of Northern Ireland is that it is part of the United Kingdom. If in the future the majority of the people of Northern Ireland should indicate a wish to become part of a united Ireland, the British Government would support that wish.

6. The conference agreed that a formal agreement incorporating the declarations of the British and Irish Governments would be signed at the formal stage of the conference and registered at the United Nations.

7. The Conference agreed that a Council of Ireland would be set up. It would be confined to representatives of the two parts of Ireland, with appropriate safeguards for the British Government's financial and other interests. It would comprise a Council of Ministers with executive and harmonising functions and a consultative role, and a consultative Assembly with advisory and review functions. The Council of Ministers would act by unanimity and would comprise a core of seven members of the Northern Ireland Executive with provision for the participation of other non-voting members of the Irish Government and Northern Ireland Executive or Administration when matters within their departmental competence were discussed. The Council of Ministers would control the functions of the Council. The Chairmanship would rotate on a basis agreed between the representatives of the Irish Government and the Northern Ireland Executive.

Arrangements would be made for the location of the first meeting, and the location of subsequent meetings would be determined by the Council of Ministers. The Consultative Assembly would consist of 60 members, 30 members from Dáil Eireann chosen by the Dáil on the basis of proportional representation by the single transferable vote, and 30 members from the Northern Ireland Assembly chosen by that Assembly and also on that basis. The members of the Consultative Assembly would be paid allowances. There would be a Secretariat to the Council, which would be kept as small as might be commensurate with efficiency in the operation of the Council. The Secretariat would serve the institutions of the Council, and would, under the Council of Ministers, supervise the carrying out of the executive and the harmonising of the functions and consultative role of the Council. The Secretariat would be headed by a Secretary-General. Following the appointment of the Northern Ireland Executive, the Irish Government and the Northern Ireland Executive would nominate their representatives to a Council of Ministers. The Council of Ministers would then appoint a Secretary-General and decide upon the location of its permanent headquarters. The Council of Ministers would also make arrangements for the recruitment of staff of the Secretariat in a manner and on conditions which would, as far as is practicable, be consistent with those applying to public servants in the two administrations.

8. In the context of its harmonising functions and consultative role, the Council of Ireland would undertake important work relating, for instance, to the impact of EEC membership. As for executive functions, the first would be to define and agree these in detail. The conference therefore decided that, in view of the administrative complexities involved, studies would at once be set in hand to identify, and, prior to the formal stage of the Conference, report on areas of common interest in relation to which a Council of Ireland would take executive decisions, and in appropriate cases, be responsible for carrying those decisions into effect. In carrying out these studies, and also in determining what should be done by the Council in terms of harmonisation, the objectives to be borne in mind would include the following:

(1) to achieve the best utilisation of scarce skills, expertise and resources

(2) to avoid, in the interests of economy and efficiency, unnecessary duplication of effort and

(3) to ensure complementary rather then competitive effort where this is to the advantage of agriculture, commerce and industry.

In particular, these studies would be directed to identifying, for the purpose of identifying for executive action by the Council of Ireland, suitable aspects of activities in the following broad fields:

(a) exploitation, conservation and development of natural resources and the environment

(b) agricultural matters (including agricultural research, animal health and operational aspects of the Common Agricultural Policy), forestry and fisheries

(c) co-operative ventures in the fields of trade and industry

(d) electricity generation

(e) tourism

(f) roads and transport

(g) advisory services in the field of public health

(h) sport, culture and the arts.

It would be for the Oireachtas and the Northern Ireland Assembly to legislate from time to time as to the extent of functions to be devolved to the Council of Ireland. Where necessary, the British Government will co-operate in this devolution of functions. Initially, the functions to be vested would be those identified in accordance with the procedures set out above and decided, at the formal stage of the Conference, to be transferred.

9. (i) During the initial period following the establishment of the Council the revenue of the Council would be provided by means of grants from the two administrations in Ireland towards agreed projects and budgets, according to the nature of the service involved.

(ii) It was also agreed that further studies would be put in hand forthwith and completed as soon as possible of methods of financing the Council after the initial period which would be consonant with the responsibilities and functions assigned to it.

(*iii*) It was agreed that the cost of the Secretariat of the Council of Ireland would be shared equally, and other services would be financed broadly in proportion to where the expenditure or benefit accrues.

(*iv*) The amount of money required to finance the Council's activities will depend upon the functions assigned to it from time to time.

(*v*) While Britain continues to pay subsidies to Northern Ireland, such payments would not involve Britain participating in the Council, it being accepted nevertheless that it would be legitimate for Britain to safeguard in an appropriate way her financial involvement in Northern Ireland.

10. It was agreed by all parties that persons committing crimes of violence, however motivated, in any part of Ireland should be brought to trial irrespective of the part of Ireland in which they are located. The concern which large sections of the people of Northern Ireland felt about this problem was in particular forcefully expressed by the representatives of the Unionist and Alliance parties. The representatives of the Irish Government stated that they understood and fully shared this concern. Different ways of solving this problem were discussed; among them were the amendment of legislation operating in the two jurisdictions on extradition, the creation of a common law enforcement area in which an all-Ireland court would have jurisdiction, and the extension of the jurisdiction of domestic courts so as to enable them to try offences committed outside the jurisdiction. It was agreed that problems of considerable legal complexity were involved, and that the British and Irish governments would jointly set up a commission to consider all the proposals put forward at the Conference and to recommend as a matter of extreme urgency the most effective means of dealing with those who commit these crimes. The Irish government undertook to take immediate and effective legal steps so that persons coming within their jurisdiction and accused of murder, however motivated, committed in Northern Ireland, will be brought to trial. And it was agreed that any similar reciprocal action that may be needed in Northern Ireland be taken by the appropriate authorities.

11. It was agreed that the Council would be invited to consider in what way the principles of the European Convention on Human Rights and Fundamental Freedom would be expressed in domestic legislation in each part of Ireland. It would recommend whether further legislation or the creation of other institutions, administrative or judicial, is required in either part or embracing the whole island to provide additional protection in the field of human rights. Such recommendations could include the functions of an Ombudsman or Commissioner for Complaints, or other arrangements of a similar nature which the Council of Ireland might think appropriate.

12. The Conference also discussed the question of policing and the need to ensure public support for and identification with the police service throughout the whole community. It was agreed that no single set of proposals would achieve those aims overnight, and that time would be necessary. The Conference expressed the hope that the wide range of agreement that had been reached, and the consequent formation of a power-sharing Executive, would make a major contribution to the creation of an atmosphere throughout the community where there would be widespread support for and identification with all the institutions of Northern Ireland.

13. It was broadly accepted that the two parts of Ireland are to a considerable extent inter-dependent in the whole field of law and order, and that the problems of political violence and identification with the police service cannot be achieved without taking into account that fact.

14. Accordingly, the British Government stated that as soon as the security problems were resolved and the new institutions were seen to be working effectively, they would wish to discuss the devolution of the responsibility for normal policing and how this might be achieved with the Northern Ireland Executive and the Police.

15. With a view to improving policing throughout the island and developing community identification with and support for the police service, the governments will co-operate under the

auspices of a Council of Ireland through their respective police authorities. To this end the Irish Government would set up a Police Authority, appointments to which would be made after consultation with the Council of Ministers of the Council of Ireland. In the case of the Northern Ireland Police Authority, appointments would be made after consultation with the Northern Ireland Executive, which would consult with the Council of Ministers of the Council of Ireland. When the two police authorities are constituted, they will make their own arrangements to achieve the objects set out above.

16. An independent complaints procedure for dealing with complaints against the police will be set up.

17. The Secretary of State for Northern Ireland will set up an all-party committee from the Assembly to examine how best to introduce effective policing throughout Northern Ireland with particular reference to the need to achieve public identification with the police.

18. The Conference took note of the reaffirmation by the British Government of their firm commitment to bring detention to an end in Northern Ireland for all sections of the community as soon as the security situation permits, and noted also that the Secretary of State for Northern Ireland hopes to be able to bring into use his statutory power of selective release in time for a number of detainees to be released before Christmas.

19. The British Government stated that, in the light of the decisions reached at the Conference, they would now seek the authority of Parliament to devolve full powers to the Northern Ireland Executive and Northern Ireland Assembly as soon as possible. The formal appointment of the Northern Ireland Executive would then be made.

20. The Conference agreed that a formal conference would be held early in the New Year at which the British and Irish Governments and the Northern Ireland Executive would meet together to consider reports on the studies which have been commissioned and to sign the agreement reached.

APPENDIX B

MEMBERS OF THE NORTHERN IRELAND ASSEMBLY

Because the parties of the United Ulster Unionist Council were operating a partial boycott of the Assembly, the house divided only once. This was the fateful division of 14 May 1974 which was used as the trigger for the start of the UWC strike the following day. Since Official Unionists were found on both government and opposition benches, I have listed members according to how they voted that day in order to lay bare the division between those who were supporting the Sunningdale Agreement and the power-sharing Executive and those who were against.

The following forty-four supported the Executive and the Sunningdale Agreement in the vote:

Norman Agnew, M.Sc., M.A., Ph.D. (Official Unionist, East Belfast)

John Lawson Baxter, B.A., B.Comm., LL.M. (Official Unionist, North Antrim)

The Rt Hon. Roy Hamilton Bradford, B.A. (Official Unionist, East Belfast)

Brigadier Ronald Joseph Callender Broadhurst (Official Unionist, South Down)

Capt. The Rt Hon. Viscount Brookeborough, D.L. (Official Unionist, North Down)

William Steven Brownlow, D.L. (Official Unionist, North Down)

Robert Victor Campbell, Ph.C., M.P.S. (Official Unionist, North Down)

Michael William E. Canavan (Social Democratic & Labour, Londonderry)

Joshua Cardwell (Official Unionist, East Belfast)

Ivan Averill Cooper, B.Sc. (Social Democratic & Labour, Mid Ulster)

Robert George Cooper, LL.B. (Alliance, West Belfast)

Derrick Samuel Frederick Crothers, M.A.(Oxon), Ph.D. (Alliance, South Antrim)

Joseph Austin Currie, B.A. (Social Democratic & Labour, Fermanagh & South Tyrone)

Thomas Anthony Daly (Social Democratic & Labour, Fermanagh & South Tyrone)

Patrick Joseph Devlin (Social Democratic & Labour, West Belfast)

Patrick Aloysius Duffy, B.A., LL.B. (Social Democratic & Labour, Mid-Ulster)

Lord Dunleath, T.D., D.L. (Alliance North Down)

Nelson Elder (Official Unionist, South Belfast)

The Rt Hon. Arthur Brian Dean Faulkner, D.L. (Official Unionist, South Down)

Frank Feely, B.A., H.Dip.Ed. (Social Democratic & Labour, South Down)

John Ferguson (Alliance, North Belfast)

Gerard Fitt, MP (Social Democratic & Labour, North Belfast)

Desmond Edward Gillespie (Social Democratic & Labour, West Belfast)

John Basil Caldwell Glass, LL.B. (Alliance, South Belfast)

Major Robert Lloyd Hall-Thompson, E.R.D., T.D. (Official Unionist, North Belfast)

John Hume, M.A. (Social Democratic & Labour, Londonderry)

The Rt Hon. Herbert Victor Kirk, B.Comm.Sc., F.C.A. (Official Unionist, South Belfast)

Aiden Joseph Larkin, M.A. (Social Democratic & Labour, Mid Ulster)

Hugh Anthony Logue (Social Democratic & Labour, Londonderry)

Edward Vincent McCloskey (Social Democratic & Labour, South Antrim)

Robert Dodd McConnell (Alliance, North Down)

Edward Kevin McGrady, F.C.A. (Social Democratic & Labour, South Down)

The Rt Hon. William Basil McIvor, LL.B., Barrister at Law (Official Unionist, South Belfast)

Peter John McLachlan, M.A. (Official Unionist, South Antrim)

Reginald Arthur Edward Magee, M.B., FRCS, CRCOG (Official Unionist, South Belfast)
Seamus Francis Mallon (Social Democratic & Labour, Armagh)
Leslie James Morrell, B.Agr. (Unionist, Londonderry)
Oliver John Napier, LL.B. (Alliance, East Belfast)
Hugh News, Ph.C., M.P.S. (Social Democratic & Labour, Armagh)
Patrick O'Donoghue (Social Democratic & Labour, South Down)
John Joseph O'Hagan, A.C.T. (Social Democratic & Labour, North Antrim)
Patrick Michael O'Hanlon, B.Comm. (Social Democratic & Labour, Armagh)
Thomas Duncan Pollock (Official Unionist, Mid Ulster)
Hugh Wilson, M.B., FRCS (Alliance, North Antrim)

The following twenty-eight voted against the Sunningdale agreement and the Executive:

Capt. Robert Austin Ardill (Official Unionist, South Antrim)
Ernest Austin Baird, Ph.C., M.P.S. (Vanguard Unionist, Fermanagh & South Tyrone)
Rev. William John Beattie (Democratic Unionist, South Antrim)
Thomas Edward Burns (Democratic Unionist, South Belfast)
Thomas Edward Carson, M.B. (Vanguard Unionist, Armagh)
Mrs Shena Elizabeth Conn, B.D.S. (Official Unionist, Londonderry)
Miss Rose Jean Coulter (Official Unionist, West Belfast)
James Craig (Democratic Unionist, North Antrim)
The Rt Hon. William Craig (Vanguard Unionist, North Antrim)
William Albert Boyd Douglas (Official Unionist, Londonderry)
John Dunlop (Vanguard Unionist, Mid Ulster)
Cecil Harvey (Vanguard Unionist, South Down)
Herbert John Heslip (Official Unionist, South Down)
Douglas Hutchinson (Democratic Unionist, Armagh)
James Alexander Kilfedder, B.A., Barrister at Law, MP (Official Unionist, North Down)
John Lunn Laird (Official Unionist, West Belfast)
Prof. Kennedy Lindsay, B.A., Ph.D. (Vanguard Unionist, South Antrim)
John McQuade (Democratic Unionist, North Belfast)
Frank Millar (Protestant & Unionist, North Belfast)

The Rt Hon. William James Morgan (Official Unionist, North Belfast)

Mrs Eileen Emily Paisley (Democratic Unionist, East Belfast)

Rev. Dr Ian Richard Kyle Paisley, MP (Democratic Unionist, North Antrim)

Charles Boucher Poots (Democratic Unionist, North Down)

James Mathew Stronge, M.A. (Official Unionist, Armagh)

The Rt Hon. John David Taylor, B.Sc. (Official Unionist, Fermanagh & South Tyrone)

William John Thompson (Official Unionist, Mid Ulster)

The Rt Hon. Henry William West (Official Unionist, Fermanagh & South Tyrone)

Herbert Whitten (Official Unionist, Armagh)

Five people did not vote:

Mr Nat Minford who as Speaker would normally not vote.

Mr David Bleakley and Mrs Anne Dickson, both Executive supporters, abstained because they were unhappy with the Council of Ireland.

Mr Glen Barr and Mr Hugh Smyth were visiting the Maze Prison at the time and were not present. Both would have voted against the Executive.

APPENDIX C

SAMPLE OF MINUTES OF THE UWC CO-ORDINATING COMMITTEE

To give an idea of how the UWC functioned, here is a copy of the minutes of a meeting of the co-ordinating committee of Thursday 23 May 1974, approximately halfway through the strike and three days after the formation of the smaller co-ordinating body at the very centre of the strike. Note that voting rights were still being settled; that there is an implication that they knew why the army were collecting samples of their passes; that republican (Catholic) areas were to get minimum fuel supplies; that they used indirect methods for controlling economic activity in areas where the strike was being flouted, mostly Catholic or mixed districts; that police were operating against them but they put their hopes on negotiation; and that taximen were to have their prices controlled. (Small wonder those taxis brave enough to travel the roads were demanding a premium.) The document was cyclo-styled for circulation on two foolscap pages and written entirely in capital letters. Names were included only where absolutely necessary. For clarification, Ballylumford was the large power station outside the port of Larne; Sandy Row and Beersbridge are Protestant areas of Belfast; Kosangas was a bottled gas company; Carryduff is a village near Belfast; the RUAS was the Royal Ulster Agricultural Society; Warrenpoint and Annalong are coastal villages in Co. Down; Dundalk is the first major town in the Republic of Ireland on the Belfast-Dublin road, and the PMG was the Postmaster General in charge of mail services.

Minutes of Co-ordinating Committee of the Ulster Workers' Council, Paramilitary and Political Organisations held at Vanguard Headquarters on Thursday 23 May 1974

On electricity it was reported that Ballylumford had four days supply.

On agriculture a member reported that it had been brought back from the brink of disaster. In some cases the army had taken the passes from drivers and another member said that some passes had been taken from drivers in Sandy Row.

It was decided that [in] view of the action taken by the army the present passes be suspended from midnight on Friday.

A new or varied pass system is being considered and while this might cause some inconvenience to some people it was due to the action of the army and was another example of how Mr Rees was disrupting community life.

At this stage a question was raised about voting rights and it was agreed that workers be entitled to three votes with one vote from each of the other organisations.

A member proposed that they should appoint a small sanctions committee to issue passes and this was passed. It was agreed that this committee should consist of Sam McClure, E. Burns, Big Billy. Sanitions sub-committee consisting of R. Pagels, Jim McIlwaine, J. Scott and Capt. Ardill was also appointed.

The chairman said three members were asked to go over to give an exclusive interview to Thames TV which had twenty million viewers and he asked for authorisation. This was passed.

A member asked about their policy towards Kosangas and it was agreed that the haulage of Kosangas should be for domestic use only, suppliers to comply with the conditions of the strike.

On the social service aspect the question was raised of the functioning of Beersbridge Post Office as otherwise they couldn't get the money out.

Another member proposed that they endorse that the workers be authorised to sort out the Giro System. This was passed.

A liaison officer gave a report on oil and fuel. He said he had tanker drivers with him at the moment who were looking after the essential services such as bread and the Milk Marketing Board creameries and these had now been supplied.

The news media had stated erroneously that hospitals were suffering but that was rubbish. Their drivers and lorries must be given excess [sic] at all barricades. They would deliver minimum amounts to Republican areas. He wanted the war council's blessing on that. Authorisation for these was given unanimously.

When the question of refuse collection was raised this was referred to the sanctions committee.

It was agreed that womenfolk be asked to come out and give the menfolk a break on the picket lines. It was also agreed to ask bands to parade in different areas from 2 p.m. onwards.

A member pointed out that the farmers' protest at Carryduff that morning had been successful and would tell the world that the farmers were with them. They would ask that this be done again on Monday and this was passed.

The committee noted that the RUAS had cancelled their annual show. They regretted the necessity for such action but thanked the society for taking such a responsible step, which would help the community in these difficult times. They expressed the hope that employers and other organisations would follow the example.

When the question of the opening hours of shops was raised it was stated that some areas operated in the usual hours and they were warned that the committee would take the matter up with wholesalers.

The same member said that the traders in Larne had been handled the wrong way and were within an ace of staging a march. He pointed out that the traders had difficulties and surely the para-military men could be more flexible.

A member said that in East Antrim police were telling petrol stations not to issue petrol to para-military men and it was agreed to draw this matter to the attention of their liasion officer.

Another member mentioned that fishing boats were being used for high profit. Apparently there were complaints about Warrenpoint. It was agreed that this was a difficult area but the chairman [said] they could stifle them by cutting off fuel.

At this stage the chairman said he had received a note from the PMG stating that all mail or none would be delivered. I have written 'none' on that note.

It was reported that two farmers in Annalong were getting their foodstuffs from Dundalk and it was decided to cut off all their fuel supplies forthwith.

In regard to taxis it was agreed that the minimum fares should be 3p and the maximum 5p.

This concluded the business.

INDEX

Agnew, Dr Norman (Official
  Unionist, East Belfast), 166
Aldergrove (Belfast) Airport, 75, 118,
  119
Allen, James, Northern Ireland
  Office, 63
Alliance Party
  coalition and compromise, 5–8,
  phasing Council of Ireland, 77,
    84, 98, 101, 102
  back-to-work marches, 84
  Wilson's ministerial broadcast, 132
  readiness to negotiate with UWC,
    143, 144, 145
  Sunningdale Agreement
    references, 159, 162
Ardill, Capt. Austin, 14, 27, 167, 170

back-to-work marches, 60, 67, 81–7,
  89, 94, 150
Baillie, Robin, 82
Baird, Ernest, 10, 24–7, 167
bakeries, 41, 56, 138, 144
Ballylumford Power Station, 54, 69,
  83, 93, 112–14, 140–43, 169
Ballymena, 115, 124, 129
Bangor, 118, 138
Barr, Andy, 38, 84
Barritt, Denis, 81, 94, 95
Baxter, John, 8, 166
BBC, 24, 27, 56, 87, 113, 152, 153
Beattie, William, 10, 58, 167
Belfast Telegraph, 81
Bloomfield, Kenneth, 118
Bogside, Derry, 76
Bradford, Rev. Robert, 60
Bradford, Roy
  Executive formation, 8
  rent and rates strike, 47
  emergency committee, 68

row over negotiation with UWC,
  73, 93, 136
Council of Ireland statement, 73
dispute over Council of Ireland
  phasing, 77–80, 96, 99
isolation within Executive, 117, 118
meeting with UDA and UVF, 118
Broadhurst, Brigadier Ronald
  (Official Unionist, South
  Down), 166
Brownlow, William Stephen (Official
  Unionist, North Down), 166
Burns, Thomas Edward (Democratic
  Unionist, South Belfast), 167

Cabinet (at Westminster)
  after state of Emergency, 70
  Law Enforcement Report, 77
  Sunningdale ratification, 79
  use of troops, 117, 128
  testing the Executive, 116, 150
  Chequers meeting with Executive
    leaders, 118, 119
  oil plan, 120, 132
Campbell, Robert Victor (Official
  Unionist, North Down), 166
Canavan, Michael (Social Democratic
  & Labour, Londonderry), 166
Cardwell, Joshua (Official Unionist,
  East Belfast), 166
Carrickfergus, 30, 110, 138
Carson, Thomas Edward (Vanguard
  Unionist, South Antrim), 167
Catherwood, Sir Fred, 144
Civil Rights Movement, 95
  NILP peace plan, 64
  re-organisation 73–4
  relations with UUUC politicians,
    74–5, 150
  back-to-work marches, 87

attitude to sanctions, 89–90
benefit payments, 92
clarification of aims, 103
oil, petrol and naphtha, 120,
139–40
threat of arrest, 126
interface with BBC, 152–3
sample minutes, 169
Confederation of Shipbuilding and
Engineering Unions, 38, 60
Conn, Mrs Shena Elizabeth (Official
Unionist, Londonderry), 167
Constitution Act, 1973, 63, 5
Coolkeeragh Power Station, 36, 54,
93, 112–15, 141
Cooper, Frank, Northern Ireland
Office, 36, 48, 73, 118
Cooper, Ivan, 8, 136, 138, 144
Cooper, Robert, 8, 77
Co-ordinating Committee (UWC)
formation, 32
meeting with Orme, 35
Cosgrave, Liam, Prime Minister of
Ireland, 101, 104
Coulter, Mrs Jean (Official Unionist,
West Belfast), 167
Council of Ireland
basić Unionist attitude, 7, 13
February 1974 general election,
16, 17
Rees ultimatum to Executive, 58, 77
NILP peace plan, 66
Bradford's opposition, 73, 79
Executive phasing sub-committee,
77–8, 80
SDLP attitude to phasing, 79–86,
96, 103–4
Devlin's change of mind, 96
near collapse of Executive,
97–103, 116
phasing and UWC, 102–3, 105
phasing and Dublin, 104
phasing and Faulknerite
backbenches, 104, 147
loyalist and UUUC view, 137,
146–7, 155
1977 stoppage, 154
Sunningdale Agreement text,
159–64

Craig, James (Democratic Unionist,
North Antrim), 10, 167
Craig, Rt Hon. William
1973 loyalist strike, 3
forms Vanguard, 5
1973 election, 6
loyalist coalition, 8, 9
meetings with UWC, 15, 26, 27
relations with Tyrie, 21
meeting with Orme, 34
meeting with Rees, 58, 59, 69
full support for stoppage, 72
later relations with UWC, 74
attitude to power sharing, 146
1977 attempted stoppage, 154
Assembly vote, 168
Creggan (Derry), 76
Crothers, Dr Derrick (Alliance, South
Antrim), 102, 166
Currie, Austin
formation of Executive, 8
Tyrie's opinion of, 13
rent and rates strike dilemma,
46–8
tribute to Faulkner, 99
SDLP resignation threat, 136
Cushendall, 71

Daly, Thomas Anthony (Social
Democratic & Labour,
Fermanagh & South Tyrone),
166
Darlington conference, 7
Democratic Unionist Party (DUP).
See also Rev. Ian Paisley
split with Unionist Party, 5
initial meetings with UWC, 15
meeting with Rees, 58
relations with UWC, 74, 75
Devlin, Paddy
formation of Executive, 8
rent and rates strike, 48
resignation letter, 48, 50
relations within SDLP, 49, 50
unemployment benefit payments,
57
Council of Ireland phasing, 77–8,
96, 101
strain on social services, 81, 90–92

Devlin, Paddy *continued*
  oil plan, 128, 134, 135
  Dublin journey, 136, 138, 144
Donaldson, Lord, 134
Dublin
  Sunningdale Agreement, 7, 8
  Tyrie's fears, 13
  February 1974 election, 16
  Loyalist bombing of, 50–52, 58, 63
  Hume, Orme and Faulkner phone
    calls, 101
  attitude to the UK, 104, 117, 156–7
  Devlin & Cooper journey, 135,
    136, 138, 144
  RTE radio, 152
  Anglo–Irish Agreement, 155
Duffy, Patrick Aloysius (Social
    Democratic & Labour, Mid
    Ulster), 166
Dundalk, 169, 171
Dungannon, 52, 115, 124
Dunleath, Lord, 102, 166
Dunlop, John (Vanguard Unionist,
    Mid Ulster), 167

Elder, Nelson (Official Unionist,
    South Belfast), 143, 166
electricity (Northern Ireland
    Electricity Service, NIES)
  Kelly's tactic, 15
  influence of British miners, 18
  Murray's view, 19, 23
  Tyrie's view, 22, 23
  Baird's outline of UWC tactic, 25–6
  Larne's importance, 30
  first day of stoppage, 34
  government response, 36
  supposed UWC/government
    agreement about, 37, 59
  second day of stoppage, 40, 41
  Maydown and Coolkeeragh battle
    53–4
  Belfast power stations close, 54, 55
  north/south link, 55
  technical staff, 60, 125
  state of emergency, 70
  danger of sudden collapse, 81, 93,
    112, 127, 140–42
  division of grid, 93

  battle over Hume's plan, 112–15,
    141
  British Cabinet view, 119
  safety concerns, 141
  Sunningdale Agreement
    provision, 161
Engineering Employers Association, 40
Executive, membership of, 8

Faulkner, Rt Hon. Brian
  proroguing of old Stormont, 4
  split in old Unionist Party, 6, 7
  Sunningdale Agreement, 7, 158
  the Executive, 8
  Unionist Party rejection, 8, 9
  Council of Ireland, 17, 96, 97, 102
  division vote in Assembly, 25
  against Sinn Féin legalisation, 33
  initial statement against UWC, 37
  Economic Council, 43
  angry with Rees, 43–4, 149
  Dublin bombings, 50
  attitude to security powers, 69
  differences with Bradford, 73, 80
  Law Enforcement Report
    problems, 77, 116
  worries about the army, 88
  situation report to assembly, 93
  near collapse of Executive,
    98–104
  summoned to Chequers, 118–19
  ministerial broadcast, 132–3
  final civil service advice, 143–4
  resignation, 144
Feather, Vic, 85
Feely, Frank (Social Democratic &
    Labour, South Down), 166
Ferguson, John (Alliance, North
    Belfast), 166
Fianna Fáil Party, 104, 117
Fine Gael Party, 117
Fitt, Gerry
  SDLP leader, 5
  Deputy Chief Executive, 8
  impact of achieving office, 12
  February 1974 general election,
    16, 147
  presses for action against
    stoppage, 44, 149

Devlin resignation letter, 48
SDLP party meeting in
    Cushendall, 71
differences with Bradford, 73
rising pessimism, 76, 77
back-to-work marches fail, 87
phasing Council of Ireland, 96
hostile party reaction to phasing,
    97–103
near collapse of Executive,
    98, 119
meeting at Chequers, 119
exasperation with Northern
    Ireland office, 134–5
SDLP resignation letter, 135, 136,
    140
Lynch phones, 135
effect of Wilson's speech, 137
FitzGerald, Garret, 101

general election February 1974, 15,
    16, 18, 79, 103, 147
Gillespie, Desmond Edward (Social
    Democratic & Labour, West
    Belfast), 166
Glass, Basil (Alliance, South Belfast),
    166
Graham, Jimmy, trade union leader,
    84, 85
grain mills, 13, 138, 150

Hall-Thompson, Major Robert
    (Official Unionist, North
    Belfast), 8, 102, 166
Harland and Wolff shipyard
    association with Harry Murray,
        14, 19
    unpreparedness for strike, 18
    largest employer, 19
    first day of strike, 28
    back-to-work march, 60, 82, 83,
        85, 87
Harvey, Cecil (Vanguard Unionist,
    South Down), 10, 167
Hayward, Ron, 122
Heath, Edward, 16, 36, 93, 94, 129
Heslip, Herbert John (Official
    Unionist, South Down), 167
Holywood, 138

Hull, Cecil, Loyalist Association of
    Workers (LAW), 13. *See also*
    LAW
Hume, John
    Executive formation, 8
    Tyrie's view of, 13
    to be blamed for power cuts, 26, 34
    associated with Orme, 36
    Economic Council, 43
    Maydown electricity battle, 54
    demands better government
        organisation, 68
    worries over government security,
        69
    row with Bradford, 73, 136
    Council of Ireland phasing, 77,
        78, 98, 199, 101
    warns of electricity supply
        collapse, 81
    electricity grid divided, 93, 115
    the oil plan, 108–11
    battle with electricity service,
        112–15, 141–3
    Wilson's broadcast reaction, 132
    drafts SDLP resignation letter, 135
    vote in assembly, 166
Hutchinson, Douglas (Democratic
    Unionist, Armagh), 10, 167
Hutchinson Yarns, Maydown, 53, 54

ICI, 30, 40, 107
Internment (detention without trial),
    7, 46, 49
IRA (Provisional Irish Republican
    Army)
    historical context, 156
    meeting with Whitelaw, 4
    comparisons with UWC and
        loyalists, 4, 59, 65, 108, 131
    effect on Derry gas supply, 19
    UUUC policy against, 20
    Sinn Féin legalised, 33
    British army concerns, 45, 127,
        134, 140, 148
    SDLP response, 46
    fears after cross-border loyalist
        bombs, 51, 52, 63
    cross-border electricity link, 55
    murder of Rev. Bradford, 60

IRA (cont.)
 NILP memorandum, 65
 interference at Coolkeeragh power
  station, 114
 Roy Bradford's view, 118
 BBC attack, 152, 153

Kelly, Billy, 15, 18, 19, 23–5, 30, 31,
 35, 72
Kilfedder, Jim, 167
King, Sir Frank, General Officer
  Commanding (GOC)
 possibilities of sabotage, 71
 oil plan pre-conditions, 110, 111,
  117, 120
Kirk, Rt Hon. Herbert, 8, 47, 166

Laird, John, 24, 34, 167
Larkin, Aiden Joseph (Social
  Democratic & Labour, Mid
  Ulster), 166
LAW (Loyalist Association of
  Workers)
 historical context, 13, 14, 18
 Andy Tyrie's view, 21, 22
Lennox, Alison (oil refinery), 107,
 108, 138, 139
Lindsay, Professor Kennedy, 10, 167
Lisburn, 52, 94, 138
Logue, Hugh (Social Democratic &
  Labour, Londonderry), 166
Lynch, Jack, 101, 104, 135
Lyttle, Tommy, 35, 75

McCahon, Joe, Ulster Farmers'
  Union, 56
McCloskey, Edward Vincent (Social
  Democratic & Labour, South
  Antrim), 166
McClure, Nonie, 95, 121
McConnell, Robert Dodd (Alliance,
  North Down), 166
McGrady, Edward, 10, 166
McGuigan, Brian, 63, 95
McIldoon, Douglas, 63, 64, 81
McIlwaine, Jim, UWC, 29, 170
McIvor, Basil, 10, 166
McKelvie, Rev. Derek, 95, 122
McLachlan, Peter, 38, 63, 82, 93, 166
McNamara, Kevin, 121, 122

McQuade, John (Democratic Unionist,
  North Belfast), 10, 167
Magee, Reginald Arthur Edward
  Magee (Official Unionist,
  South Belfast), 166
Mallon, Seamus, 79, 93, 166
Mason, Roy, 119, 134, 154
Maydown industrial complex, 36, 37,
 53
Milk Marketing Board, 41, 57, 170
Millar, Frank (Protestant & Unionist,
  North Belfast), 10, 167
Milne, Professor Alan, 81, 95, 121
Monaghan, 51, 58
Morgan, Rt Hon. William James
  (Official Unionist, North
  Belfast), 167
Morrell, Leslie, 8, 57, 77, 78, 166
Murray, Harry
 calls the stoppage, 1–3
 beginnings of UWC, 14, 24
 worry about tactics, 15
 meeting with Rees, 18
 friction with Billy Kelly, 18–19, 23
 involving oil, 19
 paramilitary connection, 22, 30
 BBC, 24, 27, 153
 Baird's assembly speech, 25
 altercation with loyalist
  politicians, 26, 27
 first day of strike, 27, 28
 meeting with Orme, 35, 36
 back-to-work marches, 83, 86
 NILP memorandum, 95
 vetting with UWC passes, 105
 closes Belfast harbour, 106
Murray, Len (Trade Union Congress),
 60, 81, 83–5, 87

Napier, Oliver
 political stance, 5
 Executive position, 8
 near collapse of Executive,
  98–102
 summoned to Chequers, 118, 119
 strategic outlook, 119
 Prime Minister's broadcast, 135
 position on negotiation, 143
 Assembly vote, 166

Prime Minister's broadcast, 135
position on negotiation, 143
Assembly vote, 166
New Ulster Movement, 63, 94, 95,
    150
News, Hugh (Social Democratic &
    Labour, Armagh), 167
Newtownards, 73, 139
NIES see electricity
Northern Ireland Civil Service, 12,
    43, 73, 87, 111, 143–4, 146
Northern Ireland Economic Council,
    43
Northern Ireland Electricity Service
    see electricity

O'Donoghue, Patrick (Social
    Democratic & Labour, South
    Down), 167
Official Unionist Party. See also
    Harry West
    local election confusion, 6
    controls party headquarters, 8–9
    UUUC formation, 9
    public support for stoppage, 71
    Assembly vote, 166
O'Hagan, John Joseph (Social
    Democratic & Labour, North
    Antrim), 167
O'Hanlon, Michael Patrick (Social
    Democratic & Labour,
    Armagh), 167
Oil Industry Emergency Committee
    (OIEC), 107, 109, 120
oil plan
    text of government oil plan,
        108–11
    Executive threat to resign en bloc,
        117
    Bradford accused, 118
    Cabinet go-ahead, 118–19, 120
    UWC counter plan, 120
    Rees hears the alternative, 123
    vacillation over implementation,
        127, 128
    Wilson's broadcast, 132
    SDLP ultimatum, 136
    implemented, 138–40
oil refinery, Belfast, 19, 138, 139

Omagh, 24, 41, 124
Orme, Stan
    Northern Ireland Office position,
        33
    meets loyalist and UWC leaders,
        33–7
    regard for trade union view, 38, 60
    initial view of use of army, 45
    outlines cost to parliament, 45
    NILP proposals, 63, 66
    re-organisation at Stormont, 68
    meets Chief Constable and GOC,
        71
    addresses SDLP at Stormont,
        99–101
    warning from Fitt, 134–6
    SDLP resignation letter, 136
Orr, Captain Lawrence, MP, South
    Down, 45

Pagels, Bob
    at Stormont, 24
    row with loyalist politicians, 26, 27
    animal feed mills, 29
    Sirocco works action, 29
    meeting with Orme, 35–6
    confusion over electricity, 72
    'Minister of agriculture', 90
    UWC minute, 170
Paisley, Rev. Ian
    Unionist Party splits, 5
    Assembly election result, 6
    UUUC coalition formed, 9
    fracas in assembly, 9–10
    formation of UWC, 15
    Tyrie's view of, 21
    learns of strike plans, 24
    row with UWC, 26, 27
    meeting with Orme, 34
    full support for strike, 72
    uneasy relationship with UWC,
        74, 75
    opposes Tyrie, 89
    predicts Executive collapse, 103
    Commons clash with Rees, 125
    1977 stoppage fails, 154
    Assembly vote, 167
Patterson, Harry (UWC), 18, 24, 26,
    27, 35

Patterson, Hugo (Electricity Service), 113
Petrie, Hugh, 13, 14, 24
police
    remove loyalists from assembly, 10
    barricade clearance, 30, 42, 44, 88
    UDA strategy against, 31, 83
    Executive doubts, 68
    separation from local control, 69
    South Armagh situation, 76
    SDLP aims, 78
    UDA confrontation in Larne, 80
    back-to-work marches, 83, 84
    total strength, 83, 149
    confrontation at Ballybeen, 88–9
    limitation of power, 142, 148
    1977 strike, 154
    Sunningdale Agreement
        references, 163, 164
    UWC minute reference, 171
Pollock, Thomas Duncan (Official
    Unionist, Mid Ulster), 167
Poots, Charles Boucher (Democratic
    Unionist, North Down), 10, 167
Portadown, 14, 30, 40, 51, 52, 124
Post Office (postal services), 34, 41,
    81, 92, 93, 109, 170
Presbyterian Church, 38

Rees, Merlyn
    becomes Northern Ireland
        Secretary, 16
    immediate options, 16, 17
    meeting with UWC, 18
    protests from Faulkner, 43
    Devlin resignation letter, 49
    difficulties with Executive, 58
    meeting with UUUC politicians,
        58, 59
    sets out government position, 59
    back-to-work marches, 60, 81, 84,
        87
    effect of SDLP position, 66
    Stormont re-organisation, 68
    declaration of emergency, 70
    demands decision on Council of
        Ireland, 76–7, 79
    confidentiality worries, 87
    Faulkner and Fitt demand
        support, 97
    Council of Ireland disquiet, 116
    Executive leaders at Chequers,
        119
    London meeting with moderates,
        122–3
    Commons clash with Paisley, 125
    army unhappy about oil plan, 127
    Prime Minister's broadcast, 131,
        135
    opposing pressures, 134
    Fitt demands action, 134–5
    crisis meeting with Wilson, 135–6
    Faulkner's resignation, 144
    army advice, 148, 149
    public relations failure, 153
    UWC minute, 170
Reid, Martin, 63
rent and rates strike, 7, 46–8
Rowlands, David, 63

Sandy Row, Belfast, 3, 143, 169, 170
schools, effect of stoppage upon, 42
Scott, Jack, 31, 170
Scott, Sandy
    opposed to stoppage, 28
    moderates delegation, 82
    trade unions and Ulster politics,
        85
    efforts towards negotiation, 87, 95
    row with McNamara, 121
    London meeting with Rees, 122,
        123, 128
SDLP (Social Democratic & Labour
    Party)
    overall political position, 5, 6, 8,
        62–3, 66
    Assembly election, 6
    at Sunningdale, 7
    Executive representation, 8
    first time in office, 12
    Tyrie's view of, 13
    rift with Faulkner Unionists, 46
    rent and rates strike, 46–8
    Devlin's resignation letter, 48–9
    Cushendall assembly party
        meeting, 71

Council of Ireland Executive
    committee, 77–9
call for Bradford's dismissal, 80
negotiation row in assembly, 93
Council of Ireland phasing split,
    96–101, 103
near collapse of Executive,
    99–101, 103
Falls branch rejects phasing, 104
wanted army used, 130, 134–6
Wilson's speech, 132
resignation ultimatum to Rees,
    135–6, 140
phasing policy endorsed, 143
end of Executive, 153
view of BBC, 153
Sunningdale Agreement, 158
Shorts aircraft factory, Belfast, 13, 19,
    40, 105
Simms, Peter (Gamble Simms Ltd),
    81, 95
Sinn Féin, 33, 147
Sirocco engineering works, Belfast,
    29, 40
Smith, Jim (Electricity Service), 114,
    142
Social Democratic and Labour Party
    see SDLP
Stewart, Rev. John, 95, 122
Strabane, 41
Stronge, James Mathew (Official
    Unionist, Armagh), 167
Sunningdale Agreement, text,
    158–64

Tandragee, 55
Taylor, John, 24, 168
Thompson, William John (Official
    Unionist, Mid Ulster), 39, 60,
    168
Trimble, David, 127, 128
Tyrie, Andy
    paramilitary position, 12, 20–21
    view of SDLP, 13
    view of Craig, 21
    joins forces with UWC, 22
    misgivings about UWC strategy,
        22, 23, 31, 72, 83
    intimidation tactics, 31, 40, 53, 88

meeting with Orme, 35–7
avoids confrontation with security
    forces, 44, 88–9, 149
in charge of UWC sanctions, 89
co–ordinating committee
    manoeuvres, 90

UDA (Ulster Defence Association)
    see Tyrie
Ulster Army Council, 20, 31, 33–5
Ulster Farmers' Union, 56
Ulster Television, 153
Ulster Volunteer Force see UVF
Ulster Workers' Council see UWC
Unionist Party (the original), 4, 5–8,
    156
United Loyalist Council, 5
UUUC (United Ulster Unionist
    Council)
    formation, 9
    Assembly disruption, 9–11
    partial Assembly boycott, 12
    February 1974 general election,
        16
    policy drawn up, 20
    paramilitary and UWC disdain
        for, 22, 23
    filibuster in Assembly, 28
    meeting with Orme, 34
    meeting with Rees, 59
    public support for stoppage, 71,
        150
    joins UWC co-ordinating
        committee, 74
    represents farmers, 90
    await arrest, 127
    formal reply to Wilson's
        broadcast, 137
UVF (Ulster Volunteer Force)
    involved in political meetings, 20
    intimidation, 31, 33, 41
    legalised, 33
    meeting with Orme, 35
    cross–border bombings, 52
    Bradford contact, 118
    1977 stoppage, 154
UWC (Ulster Workers' Council).
    See also Harry Murray
    beginnings, 2, 13, 15, 18, 21–4

UVF *continued*
    meeting with Rees, 18
    Baird's Assembly speech, 26
    row with UUUC politicians, 27
    initial effect of stoppage, 30–31
    government refusal to negotiate,
        33–4, 63, 72, 87, 95–6, 136,
        143, 144, 151–2
    electricity strategy, 34, 54, 72,
        112–15, 140–42
    meeting with Orme, 34–7, 45, 57
    essential services list, 41
    effect on food supplies, 56–7, 80
    NILP memorandum, 64–6
    UUUC public support, 71–2, 148
    re–organisation, 71–4
    relations with UUUC leaders, 74
    issue of passes, 105–6
    oil strategy, 107–8, 118, 120–21,
        138, 139, 140
    fear of arrest, 125–6
    reaction to Wilson speech, 131–2,
        136
    BBC, 152–3
    sample minutes, 169–71

Vanguard Unionist Progressive Party
    (VUPP). *See also* William Craig
    formation, 5
    Assembly election, 6
    UUUC coalition, 9
    beginnings of UWC, 13–15, 23–4
    Deputy Leader's Assembly
        speech, 25
    meets Rees, 58

1973 strike, 63
public support for stoppage, 71
await arrest, 127
vote in Assembly, 167

West, Harry. *See also* Official
    Unionist Party
    takes over Official Unionists, 8–9
    UUUC formation 9
    beginnings of, 15, 21
    Monday Club address, 34
    meets Rees, 58
    public support for stoppage, 72
    articulates farming interests, 74,
        90
    formal reply to Wilson broadcast,
        137
    1977 stoppage, 154

White, Barry, 81
Whitelaw, William, 3, 7, 129, 146
Whitten, Herbert (Official Unionist,
    Armagh), 168
Wilson, Harold
    1973 stoppage, 3
    clash with Heath, 94
    Executive leaders at Chequers,
        118–19
    broadcast speech text, 128–31
    reaction to broadcast, 131–2, 135–7
    crisis meeting with Rees, 135,
        136
Wilson, Hugh (Alliance, North
    Belfast), 167